MznLnx

Missing Links Exam Preps

Exam Prep for

Developing Management Skills: What Great Managers Know and Do

Baldwin, Bommer, & Rubin, 1st Edition

The MznLnx Exam Prep is your link from the texbook and lecture to your exams.
The MznLnx Exam Preps are unauthorized and comprehensive reviews of your textbooks.

All material provided by MznLnx and Rico Publications (c) 2010
Textbook publishers and textbook authors do not particpate in or contribute to these reviews.

MznLnx

Rico Publications

Exam Prep for Developing Management Skills: What Great Managers Know and Do
1st Edition
Baldwin, Bommer, & Rubin

Publisher: Raymond Houge
Assistant Editor: Michael Rouger
Text and Cover Designer: Lisa Buckner
Marketing Manager: Sara Swagger
Project Manager, Editorial Production: Jerry Emerson
Art Director: Vernon Lowerui

Product Manager: Dave Mason
Editorial Assitant: Rachel Guzmanji
Pedagogy: Debra Long
Cover Image: Jim Reed/Getty Images
Text and Cover Printer: City Printing, Inc.
Compositor: Media Mix, Inc.

(c) 2010 Rico Publications
ALL RIGHTS RESERVED. No part of this work covered by the copyright may be reproduced or used in any form or by an means--graphic, electronic, or mechanical, including photocopying, recording, taping, Web distribution, information storage, and retrieval systems, or in any other manner--without the written permission of the publisher.

Printed in the United States
ISBN:

> For more information about our products, contact us at:
> Dave.Mason@RicoPublications.com
>
> For permission to use material from this text or product, submit a request online to:
> Dave.Mason@RicoPublications.com

Contents

CHAPTER 1
Personal Effectiveness — 1

CHAPTER 2
Communication — 11

CHAPTER 3
Problem Solving and Ethics — 15

CHAPTER 4
Motivation — 25

CHAPTER 5
Performance Management — 34

CHAPTER 6
Power and Influence — 43

CHAPTER 7
Leadership — 50

CHAPTER 8
Team Effectiveness and Diversity — 56

CHAPTER 9
Conflict and Negotiation — 66

CHAPTER 10
Making Change — 73

ANSWER KEY — 89

TO THE STUDENT

COMPREHENSIVE

The *MznLnx* Exam Prep series is designed to help you pass your exams. Editors at MznLnx review your textbooks and then prepare these practice exams to help you master the textbook material. Unlike study guides, workbooks, and practice tests provided by the texbook publisher and textbook authors, *MznLnx* gives you **all** of the material in each chapter in exam form, not just samples, so you can be sure to nail your exam.

MECHANICAL

The MznLnx Exam Prep series creates exams that will help you learn the subject matter as well as test you on your understanding. Each question is designed to help you master the concept. Just working through the exams, you gain an understanding of the subject--its a simple mechanical process that produces success.

INTEGRATED STUDY GUIDE AND REVIEW

MznLnx is not just a set of exams designed to test you, its also a comprehensive review of the subject content. Each exam question is also a review of the concept, making sure that you will get the answer correct without having to go to other sources of material. You learn as you go! Its the easiest way to pass an exam.

HUMOR

Studying can be tedious and dry. MznLnx's instructional design includes moderate humor within the exam questions on occassion, to break the tedium and revitalize the brain

Chapter 1. Personal Effectiveness

1. _____ , often measured as an _____ Quotient (EQ), is a term that describes the ability, capacity, skill or (in the case of the trait _____ model) a self-perceived ability, to identify, assess, and manage the emotions of one's self, of others, and of groups. Different models have been proposed for the definition of _____ and disagreement exists as to how the term should be used. Despite these disagreements, which are often highly technical, the ability _____ and trait _____ models (but not the mixed models) are enjoying considerable support in the literature and have successful applications in many different domains.

   a. Emotional intelligence
   b. A4e
   c. A Stake in the Outcome
   d. AAAI

2. _____s is a sociological term for a person's 'EQ' (Emotional Intelligence Quotient), which refers to the cluster of personality traits, social graces, communication, language, personal habits, friendliness, and optimism that mark us. _____s complement hard skills (part of a person's IQ), which are the technical requirements of a job and many such similar jobs.

   A person's _____ EQ is an important part of individual contribution to the success of an organization.

   a. Social awareness
   b. Social network analysis
   c. Social influence
   d. Soft skill

3. _____ is a term defined by the Oxford English Dictionary as an individual's 'course or progress through life '. It is usually considered to pertain to remunerative work (and sometimes also formal education.)

   The etymology of the term is somewhat ironic in that it comes from the Latin word carrera, which means race .

   a. Career planning
   b. Spatial mismatch
   c. Nursing shortage
   d. Career

4. Organizational culture is not the same as _____. It is wider and deeper concepts, something that an organization 'is' rather than what it 'has' (according to Buchanan and Huczynski.)

   _____ is the total sum of the values, customs, traditions and meanings that make a company unique.

a. Job analysis
b. Corporate culture
c. Work design
d. Path-goal theory

5.

_____ is a commonly used, yet poorly defined concept in industrial and organizational psychology, the branch of psychology that deals with the workplace. It most commonly refers to whether a person performs their job well. Despite the confusion over how it should be exactly defined, performance is an extremely important criterion that relates to organizational outcomes and success.

a. 1990 Clean Air Act
b. 28-hour day
c. 33 Strategies of War
d. Job performance

6. _____ has been described as the 'process of social influence in which one person can enlist the aid and support of others in the accomplishment of a common task'. A definition more inclusive of followers comes from Alan Keith of Genentech who said '_____ is ultimately about creating a way for people to contribute to making something extraordinary happen.'

_____ is one of the most salient aspects of the organizational context. However, defining _____ has been challenging.

a. Situational leadership
b. Leadership
c. 28-hour day
d. 1990 Clean Air Act

7. _____ comprises the actual output or results of an organization as measured against its intended outputs (or goals and objectives.)

Specialists in many fields are concerned with _____ including strategic planners, operations, finance, legal, and organizational development.

In recent years, many organizations have attempted to manage _____ using the balanced scorecard methodology where performance is tracked and measured in multiple dimensions such as:

- financial performance (e.g. shareholder return)
- customer service
- social responsibility (e.g. corporate citizenship, community outreach)
- employee stewardship

a. Organizational performance
b. A Stake in the Outcome
c. AAAI
d. A4e

8. _____ is a student-centered instructional strategy in which students collaboratively solve problems and reflect on their experiences. It was pioneered and used extensively at McMaster University, Hamilton, Ontario, Canada. Characteristics of PBL are:

- Learning is driven by challenging, open-ended problems.
- Students work in small collaborative groups.
- Teachers take on the role as 'facilitators' of learning.

Accordingly, students are encouraged to take responsibility for their group and organize and direct the learning process with support from a tutor or instructor. Advocates of PBL claim it can be used to enhance content knowledge and foster the development of communication, problem-solving, and self-directed learning skill.

a. 28-hour day
b. 33 Strategies of War
c. 1990 Clean Air Act
d. Problem-based learning

9. _____ is an educational process whereby the participant studies their own actions and experience in order to improve performance. This concept is close to learning-by-doing and teaching through examples and repetitions.

_____ is done in conjunction with others, in small groups called _____ sets or two-in, two-out team.

a. A4e
b. A Stake in the Outcome
c. AAAI
d. Action learning

10. _____ is learning that occurs as a function of observing, retaining and, in the case of imitation learning, replicating novel behavior executed by others. It is most associated with the work of psychologist Albert Bandura, who implemented some of the seminal studies in the area and initiated social learning theory. It involves the process of learning to copy or model the action of another through observing another doing it.

a. A Stake in the Outcome
b. A4e
c. AAAI
d. Observational learning

11. _____ is the theory that people learn new behavior through overt reinforcement or punishment, or via observational learning of the social actors in their environment. If people observe positive, desired outcomes in the observed behavior, they are more likely to model, imitate, and adopt the behavior themselves.

_____ is derived from the work of Gabriel Tarde (1843-1904) which proposed that social learning occurred through four main stages of limitation:

- close contact,
- imitation of superiors,
- understanding of concepts,
- role model behaviour

It consists of 3 parts observing, imitating, and reinforcements

Julian Rotter moved away from theories based on psychosis and behaviourism, and developed a learning theory. In Social Learning and Clinical Psychology (1954), Rotter suggests that the effect of behaviour has an impact on the motivation of people to engage in that specific behaviour.

a. 1990 Clean Air Act
b. Social learning theory
c. 28-hour day
d. 33 Strategies of War

12. The _____ is the identical or similar social positions and social roles as a whole that influence the individuals of a group. The _____ of an individual is the culture that he or she was educated and/or lives in, and the people and institutions with whom the person interacts. A given _____ is likely to create a feeling of solidarity amongst its members, who are more likely to keep together, trust and help one another.
  a. 33 Strategies of War
  b. 1990 Clean Air Act
  c. Social environment
  d. 28-hour day

13. _____ describes the situation when output from (or information about the result of) an event or phenomenon in the past will influence the same event/phenomenon in the present or future. When an event is part of a chain of cause-and-effect that forms a circuit or loop, then the event is said to 'feed back' into itself.

_____ is also a synonym for:

- _____ signal; the information about the initial event that is the basis for subsequent modification of the event.
- _____ loop; the causal path that leads from the initial generation of the _____ signal to the subsequent modification of the event.

_____ is a mechanism, process or signal that is looped back to control a system within itself. Such a loop is called a _____ loop.

  a. Feedback loop
  b. Positive feedback
  c. 1990 Clean Air Act
  d. Feedback

14. In operant conditioning, _____ occurs when an event following a response causes an increase in the probability of that response occurring in the future. Response strength can be assessed by measures such as the frequency with which the response is made (for example, a pigeon may peck a key more times in the session), or the speed with which it is made (for example, a rat may run a maze faster.) The environment change contingent upon the response is called a reinforcer.
  a. Diminishing Manufacturing Sources and Material Shortages
  b. Meetings, Incentives, Conferences, and Exhibitions
  c. Historiometry
  d. Reinforcement

Chapter 1. Personal Effectiveness

15. _____ involves establishing specific, measurable and time-targeted objectives. Work on the theory of goal-setting suggests that it's an effective tool for making progress by ensuring that participants in a group with a common goal are clearly aware of what is expected from them if an objective is to be achieved. On a personal level, setting goals is a process that allows people to specify then work towards their own objectives - most commonly with financial or career-based goals.

    a. Digital strategy
    b. Catfish effect
    c. Resource-based view
    d. Goal setting

16. The _____ is a paradox in which a group of people collectively decide on a course of action that is counter to the preferences of any of the individuals in the group. It involves a common breakdown of group communication in which each member mistakenly believes that their own preferences are counter to the group's and, therefore, does not raise objections.

    a. AAAI
    b. A Stake in the Outcome
    c. Abilene paradox
    d. A4e

17. _____ is purposeful and reflective judgment about what to believe or what to do in response to observations, experience, verbal or written expressions, or arguments. _____ might involve determining the meaning and significance of what is observed or expressed, or, concerning a given inference or argument, determining whether there is adequate justification to accept the conclusion as true. Hence, Fisher ' Scriven define _____ as 'Skilled, active, interpretation and evaluation of observations, communications, information, and argumentation.' Parker ' Moore define it more narrowly as the careful, deliberate determination of whether one should accept, reject, or suspend judgment about a claim and the degree of confidence with which one accepts or rejects it.

    a. Virtual team
    b. Kanban
    c. Risk management
    d. Critical thinking

18. _____ is something that a firm can do well and that meets the following three conditions:

Competencies are things that companys execute well across several business units or product sectors.

Firms usually have few competencies, but these are usually less liable to change rapidly.

1. It provides consumer benefits
2. It is not easy for competitors to imitate
3. It can be leveraged widely to many products and markets.

A _____ can take various forms, including technical/subject matter know-how, a reliable process and/or close relationships with customers and suppliers (Mascarenhas et al. 1998.)

   a. Dominant Design
   b. Learning-by-doing
   c. NAIRU
   d. Core competency

19. _____, cultural quotient or CQ, is a theory within management and organisational psychology, positing that understanding the impact of an individual's cultural background on their behaviour is essential for effective business, and measuring an individual's ability to engage successfully in any environment or social setting. First described by Christopher Earley and Soon Ang in _____: Individual Interactions Across Cultures. The book was published in 2003 by Stanford University.
   a. Free cash flow
   b. Sole proprietorship
   c. Time to market
   d. Cultural intelligence

20. _____ is one of five major domains of personality discovered by psychologists. Openness involves active imagination, aesthetic sensitivity, attentiveness to inner feelings, preference for variety, and intellectual curiosity. A great deal of psychometric research has demonstrated that these qualities are statistically correlated.
   a. Introversion
   b. Introverts
   c. Extraversion
   d. Openness to experience

21. In psychology, _____ is a major approach to the study of human personality. Trait theorists are primarily interested in the measurement of traits, which can be defined as habitual patterns of behavior, thought, and emotion. According to this perspective, traits are relatively stable over time, differ among individuals (e.g. some people are outgoing whereas others are shy), and influence behavior.
   a. Psychometrics
   b. Trait theory
   c. Psychological statistics
   d. Cognitive dissonance

22. The _____ assessment is a psychometric questionnaire designed to measure psychological preferences in how people perceive the world and make decisions.[1] These preferences were extrapolated from the typological theories originated by Carl Gustav Jung, as published in his 1921 book Psychological Types. The original developers of the personality inventory were Katharine Cook Briggs and her daughter, Isabel Briggs Myers. They began creating the indicator during World War II, believing that a knowledge of personality preferences would help women who were entering the industrial workforce for the first time identify the sort of war-time jobs where they would be 'most comfortable and effective'.[xiii] The initial questionnaire grew into the _____, which was first published in 1962.

  a. 33 Strategies of War
  b. Myers-Briggs Type Indicator
  c. 1990 Clean Air Act
  d. 28-hour day

23. A _____ is a set of consistent ethic values (more specifically the personal and cultural values) and measures used for the purpose of ethical or ideological integrity. A well defined _____ is a moral code.

Fred Wenst>øp and Arild Myrmel have proposed a structure for corporate _____s that consists of three value categories. These are considered complementary and juxtaposed on the same level if illustrated graphically on for instance an organization's web page. The first value category is Core Values, which prescribe the attitude and character of an organization, and are often found in sections on Code of conduct on its web page. The philosophical antecedents of these values are Virtue ethics, which is often attributed to Aristotle. Protected Values are protected through rules, standards and certifications. They are often concerned with areas such as health, environment and safety. The third category, Created Values, is the values that stakeholders, including the shareholders expect in return for their contributions to the firm. These values are subject to trade-off by decision-makers or bargaining processes. This process is explained further in Stakeholder theory.

  a. 1990 Clean Air Act
  b. 28-hour day
  c. 33 Strategies of War
  d. Value system

24. _____ is one of the managerial functions like planning, organizing, staffing and directing. It is an important function because it helps to check the errors and to take the corrective action so that deviation from standards are minimized and stated goals of the organization are achieved in desired manner. According to modern concepts, _____ is a foreseeing action whereas earlier concept of _____ was used only when errors were detected. _____ in management means setting standards, measuring actual performance and taking corrective action.

  a. Schedule of reinforcement
  b. Control
  c. Turnover
  d. Decision tree pruning

Chapter 1. Personal Effectiveness

25. The _____ captures an expanded spectrum of values and criteria for measuring organizational success: economic, ecological and social. With the ratification of the United Nations and ICLEI _____ standard for urban and community accounting in early 2007, this became the dominant approach to public sector full cost accounting. Similar UN standards apply to natural capital and human capital measurement to assist in measurements required by _____, e.g. the ecoBudget standard for reporting ecological footprint.

    a. Triple bottom line
    b. 1990 Clean Air Act
    c. 33 Strategies of War
    d. 28-hour day

26. _____ refers to a range of skills, tools, and techniques used to manage time when accomplishing specific tasks, projects and goals. This set encompass a wide scope of activities, and these include planning, allocating, setting goals, delegation, analysis of time spent, monitoring, organizing, scheduling, and prioritizing. Initially _____ referred to just business or work activities, but eventually the term broadened to include personal activities also.

    a. Cash cow
    b. Formula for Change
    c. Voice of the customer
    d. Time management

27. _____ is an action management method created by David Allen, and described in a book of the same name. Both '_____' and '_____' are registered trademarks of the David Allen Company.

    _____ rests on the principle that a person needs to move tasks out of the mind by recording them externally.

    a. Getting Things Done
    b. Business Process Improvement
    c. Middle management
    d. Distributed Development

28. _____-model (SCOR(r)) is a process reference model developed by the management consulting firm PRTM and AMR Research and endorsed by the Supply-Chain Council (SCC) as the cross-industry de facto standard diagnostic tool for supply chain management. SCOR enables users to address, improve, and communicate supply chain management practices within and between all interested parties in the Extended Enterprise.

    SCOR(r) is a management tool, spanning from the supplier's supplier to the customer's customer. The model has been developed by the members of the Council on a volunteer basis to describe the business activities associated with all phases of satisfying a customer's demand.

a. Supply-Chain Operations Reference
b. Supply Chain Risk Management
c. Supply chain management software
d. Delayed differentiation

Chapter 2. Communication

1. A _____ or business method is a collection of related, structured activities or tasks that produce a specific service or product (serve a particular goal) for a particular customer or customers. It often can be visualized with a flowchart as a sequence of activities.

There are three types of _____es:

   1. Management processes, the processes that govern the operation of a system. Typical management processes include 'Corporate Governance' and 'Strategic Management'.
   2. Operational processes, processes that constitute the core business and create the primary value stream. Typical operational processes are Purchasing, Manufacturing, Marketing, and Sales.
   3. Supporting processes, which support the core processes. Examples include Accounting, Recruitment, Technical support.

A _____ begins with a customer's need and ends with a customer's need fulfillment. Process oriented organizations break down the barriers of structural departments and try to avoid functional silos.

   a. 28-hour day
   b. Business process
   c. 1990 Clean Air Act
   d. 33 Strategies of War

2. _____ of the learning curve effect and the closely related experience curve effect express the relationship between equations for experience and efficiency or between efficiency gains and investment in the effort. The experience of 'learning curves' was first observed by the 19th Century German psychologist Hermann Ebbinghaus according to the difficulty of memorizing varying numbers of verbal stimuli, and subsequent learning about the complex processes of learning are discussed in the

The rule used for representing the learning curve effect states that the more times a task has been performed, the less time will be required on each subsequent iteration.

   a. Spatial Decision Support Systems
   b. Distribution
   c. Point biserial correlation coefficient
   d. Models

3. The term _____ is used in various contexts. For example, in business process modeling the enterprise _____ is often referred to as the business _____. Process models are core concepts in the discipline of Process Engineering.

a. 1990 Clean Air Act
b. 28-hour day
c. 33 Strategies of War
d. Process model

4. _____ is a mathematical science pertaining to the collection, analysis, interpretation or explanation, and presentation of data. It also provides tools for prediction and forecasting based on data. It is applicable to a wide variety of academic disciplines, from the natural and social sciences to the humanities, government and business.
   a. Simple moving average
   b. Failure rate
   c. Location parameter
   d. Statistics

5. _____ describes the situation when output from (or information about the result of) an event or phenomenon in the past will influence the same event/phenomenon in the present or future. When an event is part of a chain of cause-and-effect that forms a circuit or loop, then the event is said to 'feed back' into itself.

_____ is also a synonym for:

- _____ signal; the information about the initial event that is the basis for subsequent modification of the event.
- _____ loop; the causal path that leads from the initial generation of the _____ signal to the subsequent modification of the event.

_____ is a mechanism, process or signal that is looped back to control a system within itself. Such a loop is called a _____ loop.

   a. 1990 Clean Air Act
   b. Feedback loop
   c. Feedback
   d. Positive feedback

6. In operant conditioning, _____ occurs when an event following a response causes an increase in the probability of that response occurring in the future. Response strength can be assessed by measures such as the frequency with which the response is made (for example, a pigeon may peck a key more times in the session), or the speed with which it is made (for example, a rat may run a maze faster.) The environment change contingent upon the response is called a reinforcer.

a. Meetings, Incentives, Conferences, and Exhibitions
b. Diminishing Manufacturing Sources and Material Shortages
c. Historiometry
d. Reinforcement

7. _____ is a contract between two parties, one being the employer and the other being the employee. An employee may be defined as: 'A person in the service of another under any contract of hire, express or implied, oral or written, where the employer has the power or right to control and direct the employee in the material details of how the work is to be performed.' Black's Law Dictionary page 471 (5th ed. 1979.)
   a. Employment counsellor
   b. Employment
   c. Exit interview
   d. Employment rate

8. _____ is the body of laws, administrative rulings, and precedents which address the legal rights of, and restrictions on, working people and their organizations. As such, it mediates many aspects of the relationship between trade unions, employers and employees. In Canada, employment laws related to unionized workplaces are differentiated from those relating to particular individuals.
   a. Trade union
   b. Labor law
   c. Four-day week
   d. Shift work

9. _____ is the state or fact of exclusive rights and control over property, which may be an object, land/real estate or intellectual property. An _____ right is also referred to as title. The concept of _____ has existed for thousands of years and in all cultures.
   a. Emanation of the state
   b. A4e
   c. Ownership
   d. A Stake in the Outcome

10. An _____ is an overview of an idea for a product, service, or project. The name reflects the fact that an _____ can be delivered in the time span of an elevator ride (for example, thirty seconds and 100-150 words).

The term is typically used in the context of an entrepreneur pitching an idea to a venture capitalist or angel investor to receive funding.

a. AAAI
b. A Stake in the Outcome
c. Elevator pitch
d. A4e

11. _____ is a trait taught by many personal development experts and psychotherapists and the subject of many popular self-help books. It is linked to self-esteem and considered an important communication skill.

As a communication style and strategy, _____ is distinguished from aggression and passivity.

a. A4e
b. A Stake in the Outcome
c. Intrinsic motivation
d. Assertiveness

Chapter 3. Problem Solving and Ethics

1. _____ can be regarded as an outcome of mental processes (cognitive process) leading to the selection of a course of action among several alternatives. Every _____ process produces a final choice. The output can be an action or an opinion of choice.
   a. 1990 Clean Air Act
   b. Decision making
   c. 33 Strategies of War
   d. 28-hour day

2. A _____ is a job interview in which the applicant is given a question/situation/problem/challenge and asked to resolve the situation. The case problem is often a business situation or a business case that the interviewer has worked on in real life.

   After the applicant is given information about the case, the applicant is expected to ask the interviewer logical and sequential questions that will enable the applicant to understand the situation, probe deeper into relevant areas, gather pertinent information and arrive at a solution or recommendation for the question or situation at hand.

   a. Case interview
   b. Duties of directors
   c. Situational judgement tests
   d. Decision tree pruning

3. _____ consists of the mental process of thinking involved with the process of judging the merits of multiple options and selecting one of them for action. Some simple examples include deciding whether to get up in the morning or go back to sleep, or selecting a given route for a journey. More complex examples (often decisions that affect what a person thinks or their core beliefs) include choosing a lifestyle, religious affiliation, or political position.
   a. Choice
   b. Trade study
   c. Groups decision making
   d. Championship mobilization

4. In attribution theory, the _____ is a theory describing cognitive tendency to predominantly over-value dispositional explanations for the observed behaviors of others, thus under-valuing or acknowledging the potentiality of situational attributions or situational explanations for the behavioral motives of others. In other words, people predominantly presume that the actions of others are indicative of the 'kind' of person they are, rather than the kind of situations that compels their behavior. However, the over attribution effect generally does not account for our own ability to self-justify our behaviors; we tend to prefer interpreting our own actions in terms of the situational variables accessible to our awareness.

a. Pygmalion effect
b. Halo effect
c. Confirmation bias
d. Fundamental attribution error

5. A _____ occurs when people attribute their successes to internal or personal factors but attribute their failures to situational factors beyond their control. The _____ can be seen in the common human tendency to take credit for success but to deny responsibility for failure. It may also manifest itself as a tendency for people to evaluate ambiguous information in a way that is beneficial to their interests.
   a. Halo effect
   b. Pygmalion effect
   c. Fundamental attribution error
   d. Self-serving bias

6. _____ is a way of expressing knowledge or belief that an event will occur or has occurred. In mathematics the concept has been given an exact meaning in _____ theory, that is used extensively in such areas of study as mathematics, statistics, finance, gambling, science, and philosophy to draw conclusions about the likelihood of potential events and the underlying mechanics of complex systems.

The word _____ does not have a consistent direct definition.

   a. Standard deviation
   b. Time series analysis
   c. Statistics
   d. Probability

7. _____ is a contract between two parties, one being the employer and the other being the employee. An employee may be defined as: 'A person in the service of another under any contract of hire, express or implied, oral or written, where the employer has the power or right to control and direct the employee in the material details of how the work is to be performed.' Black's Law Dictionary page 471 (5th ed. 1979.)
   a. Employment counsellor
   b. Employment
   c. Exit interview
   d. Employment rate

8. _____ is the body of laws, administrative rulings, and precedents which address the legal rights of, and restrictions on, working people and their organizations. As such, it mediates many aspects of the relationship between trade unions, employers and employees. In Canada, employment laws related to unionized workplaces are differentiated from those relating to particular individuals.
   a. Shift work
   b. Trade union
   c. Four-day week
   d. Labor law

9. In psychology and cognitive science, _____ is a tendency to search for or interpret new information in a way that confirms one's preconceptions and to irrationally avoid information and interpretations which contradict prior beliefs. _____ is a type of cognitive bias and represents an error of inductive inference, or as a form of selection bias toward confirmation of the hypothesis under study or disconfirmation of an alternative hypothesis.

_____ is of interest in the teaching of critical thinking, as the skill (of thinking critically) is misused if rigorous critical scrutiny is applied only to evidence challenging a preconceived idea but not to evidence supporting it.

   a. Self-serving bias
   b. Confirmation bias
   c. Cognitive biases
   d. Choice-supportive bias

10. _____ was first described by Barry M. Staw in his 1976 paper, 'Knee deep in the big muddy: A study of escalating commitment to a chosen course of action'. More recently the term Sunk cost fallacy has been used to describe the phenomenon where people justify increased investment in a decision, based on the cumulative prior investment, despite new evidence suggesting that the decision was probably wrong. Such investment may include money, time, or -- in the case of military strategy -- human lives.
   a. A Stake in the Outcome
   b. Open Options
   c. A4e
   d. Escalation of commitment

11. In game theory, an _____ is a set of moves or strategies taken by the players, or their payoffs resulting from the actions or strategies taken by all players. The two are complementary in that given knowledge of the set of strategies of all players, the final state of the game is known, as are any relevant payoffs. In a game where chance or a random event is involved, the _____ is not known from only the set of strategies, but is only realized when the random event(s) are realized.

Chapter 3. Problem Solving and Ethics

   a. AAAI
   b. A4e
   c. A Stake in the Outcome
   d. Outcome

12. _____ is a concept based on the fact that rationality of individuals is limited by the information they have, the cognitive limitations of their minds, and the finite amount of time they have to make decisions. This contrasts with the concept of rationality as optimization. Another way to look at _____ is that, because decision-makers lack the ability and resources to arrive at the optimal solution, they instead apply their rationality only after having greatly simplified the choices available.
   a. Mixed strategy
   b. Transferable utility
   c. Complete information
   d. Bounded rationality

13. _____ is a term used in project management and business administration to describe a process where all the individuals or groups that are likely to be affected by the activities of a project are identified and then sorted according to how much they can affect the project and how much the project can affect them. This information is used to assess how the interests of those stakeholders should be addressed in the project plan.

A stakeholder is any person or organization, who can be positively or negatively impacted by, or cause an impact on the actions of a company.

   a. 1990 Clean Air Act
   b. 33 Strategies of War
   c. 28-hour day
   d. Stakeholder analysis

14. A _____ is a decision support tool that uses a tree-like graph or model of decisions and their possible consequences, including chance event outcomes, resource costs, and utility. _____s are commonly used in operations research, specifically in decision analysis, to help identify a strategy most likely to reach a goal. Another use of _____s is as a descriptive means for calculating conditional probabilities.
   a. 33 Strategies of War
   b. 28-hour day
   c. 1990 Clean Air Act
   d. Decision tree

15. The _____ (Situation, Task, Action, Result) format is a job interview technique used by interviewers to gather all the relevant information about a specific capability that the job requires. This interview format is said to have a higher degree of predictability of future on-the-job performance than the traditional interview.

- Situation: The interviewer wants you to present a recent challenge and situation in which you found yourself.
- Task: What did you have to achieve? The interviewer will be looking to see what you were trying to achieve from the situation.
- Action: What did you do? The interviewer will be looking for information on what you did, why you did it and what were the alternatives.
- Results: What was the outcome of your actions? What did you achieve through your actions and did you meet your objectives. What did you learn from this experience and have you used this learning since?

   a. Competency-based job descriptions
   b. Rasch models
   c. Phrase completion
   d. STAR

16. The term '_____' refers to the concept of collecting information and attempting to spot a pattern in the information. In some fields of study, the term '_____' has more formally-defined meanings.

In project management _____ is a mathematical technique that uses historical results to predict future outcome.

   a. Stepwise regression
   b. Least squares
   c. Regression analysis
   d. Trend analysis

17. _____ of the learning curve effect and the closely related experience curve effect express the relationship between equations for experience and efficiency or between efficiency gains and investment in the effort. The experience of 'learning curves' was first observed by the 19th Century German psychologist Hermann Ebbinghaus according to the difficulty of memorizing varying numbers of verbal stimuli, and subsequent learning about the complex processes of learning are discussed in the

.

The rule used for representing the learning curve effect states that the more times a task has been performed, the less time will be required on each subsequent iteration.

a. Distribution
b. Spatial Decision Support Systems
c. Point biserial correlation coefficient
d. Models

18. The _____ is a business tool used to organize ideas and data. It is one of the Seven Management and Planning Tools.

The tool is commonly used within project management and allows large numbers of ideas to be sorted into groups for review and analysis.

The _____ was devised by Jiro Kawakita in the 1960s and is sometimes referred to as the KJ Method.

a. AAAI
b. A4e
c. A Stake in the Outcome
d. Affinity diagram

19. In statistics, a _____ is a graphical display of tabulated frequencies, shown as bars. It shows what proportion of cases fall into each of several categories: it is a form of data binning. The categories are usually specified as non-overlapping intervals of some variable.
a. Standard deviation
b. Histogram
c. Statistics
d. Correlation

20. _____ is a group creativity technique designed to generate a large number of ideas for the solution of a problem. The method was first popularized in the late 1930s by Alex Faickney Osborn in a book called Applied Imagination. Osborn proposed that groups could double their creative output with _____.
a. Adam Smith
b. Affiliation
c. Abraham Harold Maslow
d. Brainstorming

21. 6-3-5 _____ is a group creativity technique used in marketing, advertising, design, writing and product development originally developed by Professor Bernd Rohrbach in 1968.

Based on the concept of Brainstorming, the aim of 6-3-5 _____ is to generate 108 new ideas in half an hour. In a similar way to brainstorming, it is not the quality of ideas that matters but the quantity.

The technique involves 6 participants who sit in a group and are supervised by a moderator. Each participant thinks up 3 ideas every 5 minutes. Participants are encouraged to draw on others' ideas for inspiration, thus stimulating the creative process. After 6 rounds in 30 minutes the group has thought up a total of 108 ideas.

   a. 1990 Clean Air Act
   b. 33 Strategies of War
   c. 28-hour day
   d. Brainwriting

22. _____ describes the situation when output from (or information about the result of) an event or phenomenon in the past will influence the same event/phenomenon in the present or future. When an event is part of a chain of cause-and-effect that forms a circuit or loop, then the event is said to 'feed back' into itself.

_____ is also a synonym for:

- _____ signal; the information about the initial event that is the basis for subsequent modification of the event.
- _____ loop; the causal path that leads from the initial generation of the _____ signal to the subsequent modification of the event.

_____ is a mechanism, process or signal that is looped back to control a system within itself. Such a loop is called a _____ loop.

   a. Feedback
   b. Feedback loop
   c. 1990 Clean Air Act
   d. Positive feedback

23. In economics, collective bargaining, psychology, and political science, 'free riders' are those who consume more than their fair share of a public resource, or shoulder less than a fair share of the costs of its production. Free riding is usually considered to be an economic 'problem' only when it leads to the non-production or under-production of a public good (and thus to Pareto inefficiency), or when it leads to the excessive use of a common property resource. The _____ is the question of how to limit free riding (or its negative effects) in these situations.

Chapter 3. Problem Solving and Ethics

a. 28-hour day
b. Free rider problem
c. 1990 Clean Air Act
d. Natural monopoly

24. In the social psychology of groups, _____ is the phenomenon of people making less effort to achieve a goal when they work in a group than when they work alone. This is seen as one of the main reasons groups are sometimes less productive than the combined performance of their members working as individuals.

- Ringelmann, Max : 1913

Research began in 1913 with Max Ringelmann's study. He found that when he asked a group of men to pull on a rope, that they did not pull as hard, or put as much effort into the activity, as they did when they were pulling alone.

a. Personal space
b. Self-enhancement
c. Machiavellianism
d. Social loafing

25. _____ is the process of comparing the cost, cycle time, productivity, or quality of a specific process or method to another that is widely considered to be an industry standard or best practice. Essentially, _____ provides a snapshot of the performance of your business and helps you understand where you are in relation to a particular standard. The result is often a business case for making changes in order to make improvements.

a. Cost leadership
b. Complementors
c. Competitive heterogeneity
d. Benchmarking

26. _____ is the principle that in open systems a given end state can be reached by many potential means. The term is due to Ludwig von Bertalanffy, the founder of General Systems Theory. He prefers this term, in contrast to 'goal', in describing complex systems' similar or convergent behavior.

a. A Stake in the Outcome
b. A4e
c. AAAI
d. Equifinality

Chapter 3. Problem Solving and Ethics

27. In decision theory and estimation theory, the _____ of an estimator, $\hat{\theta}$, of an unknown parameter of the distribution, θ, is the expected value of the loss function

$$R(\theta, \hat{\theta}) = \mathbb{E}_\theta L(\theta, \hat{\theta}) = \int L(\theta, \hat{\theta})\, dP_\theta.$$

where dP_θ is a probability measure parametrized by θ.

- For a scalar parameter θ and a quadratic loss function,

$$L(\theta, \hat{\theta}) = (\theta - \hat{\theta})^2$$

the _____ function becomes the mean squared error of the estimate,

$$R(\theta, \hat{\theta}) = E_\theta(\theta - \hat{\theta})^2$$

- In density estimation, the unknown parameter is probability density itself. The loss function is typically chosen to be a norm in an appropriate function space. For example, for L^2 norm,

$$L(f, \hat{f}) = \|f - \hat{f}\|_2^2$$

the _____ function becomes the mean integrated squared error

$$R(f, \hat{f}) = E\|f - \hat{f}\|^2$$

a. Linear model
b. Risk aversion
c. Financial modeling
d. Risk

28. _____ comprises a range of practices used in an organisation to identify, create, represent, distribute and enable adoption of insights and experiences. Such insights and experiences comprise knowledge, either embodied in individuals or embedded in organisational processes or practice.

An established discipline since 1991, _____ includes courses taught in the fields of business administration, information systems, management, and library and information sciences .

a. 28-hour day
b. 1990 Clean Air Act
c. 33 Strategies of War
d. Knowledge management

29. _____ is an educational process whereby the participant studies their own actions and experience in order to improve performance. This concept is close to learning-by-doing and teaching through examples and repetitions.

_____ is done in conjunction with others, in small groups called _____ sets or two-in, two-out team.

a. A Stake in the Outcome
b. AAAI
c. Action learning
d. A4e

30. An _____ is a situation that will often involve an apparent conflict between moral imperatives, in which to obey one would result in transgressing another. This is also called an ethical paradox since in moral philosophy, paradox plays a central role in ethics debates. For instance, an ethical admonition to 'love thy neighbour as thy self' is not always just in contrast with, but sometimes in contradiction to an armed neighbour actively trying to kill you: if he or she succeeds, you will not be able to love him or her.

a. AAAI
b. A Stake in the Outcome
c. A4e
d. Ethical dilemma

31. The 'business case for _____', theorizes that in a global marketplace, a company that employs a diverse workforce (both men and women, people of many generations, people from ethnically and racially diverse backgrounds etc.) is better able to understand the demographics of the marketplace it serves and is thus better equipped to thrive in that marketplace than a company that has a more limited range of employee demographics.

An additional corollary suggests that a company that supports the _____ of its workforce can also improve employee satisfaction, productivity and retention.

a. Kanban
b. Virtual team
c. Trademark
d. Diversity

Chapter 4. Motivation

1. _____ is an attempt to motivate employees by giving them the opportunity to use the range of their abilities. It is an idea that was developed by the American psychologist Frederick Herzberg in the 1950s. It can be contrasted to job enlargement which simply increases the number of tasks without changing the challenge.
   a. Catfish effect
   b. Cash cow
   c. C-A-K-E
   d. Job enrichment

2. _____ is about the mental processes regarding choice, or choosing. It explains the processes that an individual undergoes to make choices. In organizational behavior study, _____ is a motivation theory first proposed by Victor Vroom of the Yale School of Management.
   a. A4e
   b. AAAI
   c. A Stake in the Outcome
   d. Expectancy theory

3. _____ is a commonly used, yet poorly defined concept in industrial and organizational psychology, the branch of psychology that deals with the workplace. It most commonly refers to whether a person performs their job well. Despite the confusion over how it should be exactly defined, performance is an extremely important criterion that relates to organizational outcomes and success.

   a. 28-hour day
   b. 33 Strategies of War
   c. 1990 Clean Air Act
   d. Job performance

4. Maslow's _____ is a theory in psychology, proposed by Abraham Maslow in his 1943 paper A Theory of Human Motivation, which he subsequently extended to include his observations of humans' innate curiosity.

Maslow's _____ is predetermined in order of importance. It is often depicted as a pyramid consisting of five levels: the lowest level is associated with physiological needs, while the uppermost level is associated with self-actualization needs, particularly those related to identity and purpose. Deficiency needs must be met first. Once these are met, seeking to satisfy growth needs drives personal growth. The higher needs in this hierarchy only come into focus when the lower needs in the pyramid are met.

Chapter 4. Motivation

a. 28-hour day
b. 33 Strategies of War
c. 1990 Clean Air Act
d. Hierarchy of needs

5. _____, cultural quotient or CQ, is a theory within management and organisational psychology, positing that understanding the impact of an individual's cultural background on their behaviour is essential for effective business, and measuring an individual's ability to engage successfully in any environment or social setting. First described by Christopher Earley and Soon Ang in _____: Individual Interactions Across Cultures. The book was published in 2003 by Stanford University.

a. Time to market
b. Free cash flow
c. Sole proprietorship
d. Cultural intelligence

6. In game theory, an _____ is a set of moves or strategies taken by the players, or their payoffs resulting from the actions or strategies taken by all players. The two are complementary in that given knowledge of the set of strategies of all players, the final state of the game is known, as are any relevant payoffs. In a game where chance or a random event is involved, the _____ is not known from only the set of strategies, but is only realized when the random event(s) are realized.

a. AAAI
b. A Stake in the Outcome
c. A4e
d. Outcome

7. _____ is a term that has been used in various psychology theories, often in slightly different ways (e.g., Goldstein, Maslow, Rogers.) The term was originally introduced by the organismic theorist Kurt Goldstein for the motive to realise all of one's potentialities. In his view, it is the master motive--indeed, the only real motive a person has, all others being merely manifestations of it.

a. 28-hour day
b. 1990 Clean Air Act
c. Self-actualization
d. 33 Strategies of War

8. The 'business case for _____', theorizes that in a global marketplace, a company that employs a diverse workforce (both men and women, people of many generations, people from ethnically and racially diverse backgrounds etc.) is better able to understand the demographics of the marketplace it serves and is thus better equipped to thrive in that marketplace than a company that has a more limited range of employee demographics.

Chapter 4. Motivation 27

An additional corollary suggests that a company that supports the _____ of its workforce can also improve employee satisfaction, productivity and retention.

a. Trademark
b. Kanban
c. Virtual team
d. Diversity

9. A _____ is one scenario provided for evaluation by respondents in a Choice Experiment. Responses are collected and used to create a Choice Model. Respondents are usually provided with a series of differing _____s for evaluation.

a. Computerized classification test
b. Thurstone scale
c. Pairwise comparison
d. Choice Set

10. A _____ is a process in which a potential employee is evaluated by an employer for prospective employment in their company, organization and was established in the late 16th century.

A _____ typically precedes the hiring decision, and is used to evaluate the candidate. The interview is usually preceded by the evaluation of submitted résumés from interested candidates, then selecting a small number of candidates for interviews.

a. Split shift
b. Supported employment
c. Payrolling
d. Job interview

11. _____ refers to an individual's desire for significant accomplishment, mastering of skills, control, or high standards. The term was introduced by the psychologist, David McClelland.

_____ is related to the difficulty of tasks people choose to undertake.

a. 1990 Clean Air Act
b. Need for power
c. Two-factor theory
d. Need for achievement

Chapter 4. Motivation

12. The _____ is a term that was popularised by David McClelland and describes a person's need to feel a sense of involvement and 'belonging' within a social group. However, it should be recognised that McClellend's thinking was strongly influenced by the pioneering work of Henry Murray who first identified underlying psychological human needs and motivational processes (1938.) It was Murray who set out a taxonomy of needs, including Achievement, Power and Affiliation - and placed these in the context of an integrated motivational model.
   a. SESAMO
   b. Strong-Campbell Interest Inventory
   c. Need for affiliation
   d. Polynomial conjoint measurement

13. _____ is a term that was popularized by renowned psychologist David McClelland in 1961. However, it should be recognized that McClellend's thinking was strongly influenced by the pioneering work of Henry Murray who first identified underlying psychological human needs and motivational processes (1938.) It was Murray who set out a taxonomy of needs, including Achievement, Power and Affiliation - and placed these in the context of an integrated motivational model.
   a. Two-factor theory
   b. Need for Achievement
   c. 1990 Clean Air Act
   d. Need for power

14. The _____ captures an expanded spectrum of values and criteria for measuring organizational success: economic, ecological and social. With the ratification of the United Nations and ICLEI _____ standard for urban and community accounting in early 2007, this became the dominant approach to public sector full cost accounting. Similar UN standards apply to natural capital and human capital measurement to assist in measurements required by _____, e.g. the ecoBudget standard for reporting ecological footprint.
   a. 28-hour day
   b. 1990 Clean Air Act
   c. 33 Strategies of War
   d. Triple bottom line

15. In law, _____ is the term to describe a partnership between two or more parties.

In England a number of statutes on the subject have been passed, the chief being the Bastardy Act of 1845, and the Bastardy Laws Amendment Acts of 1872 and 1873. The mother of a bastard may summon the putative father to petty sessions within twelve months of the birth (or at any later time if he is proved to have contributed to the child's support within twelve months after the birth), and the justices, as after hearing evidence on both sides, may, if the mother's evidence be corroborated in some material particular, adjudge the man to be the putative father of the child, and order him to pay a sum not exceeding five shillings a week for its maintenance, together with a sum for expenses incidental to the birth, or the funeral expenses, if it has died before the date of order, and the costs of the proceedings.

a. Affiliation
b. Adam Smith
c. Abraham Harold Maslow
d. Affiliation

16. _____ has been described as the 'process of social influence in which one person can enlist the aid and support of others in the accomplishment of a common task'. A definition more inclusive of followers comes from Alan Keith of Genentech who said '_____ is ultimately about creating a way for people to contribute to making something extraordinary happen.'

_____ is one of the most salient aspects of the organizational context. However, defining _____ has been challenging.

a. Situational leadership
b. Leadership
c. 28-hour day
d. 1990 Clean Air Act

17. The _____ is the identical or similar social positions and social roles as a whole that influence the individuals of a group. The _____ of an individual is the culture that he or she was educated and/or lives in, and the people and institutions with whom the person interacts. A given _____ is likely to create a feeling of solidarity amongst its members, who are more likely to keep together, trust and help one another.
a. 33 Strategies of War
b. 28-hour day
c. 1990 Clean Air Act
d. Social environment

18. _____ describes the situation when output from (or information about the result of) an event or phenomenon in the past will influence the same event/phenomenon in the present or future. When an event is part of a chain of cause-and-effect that forms a circuit or loop, then the event is said to 'feed back' into itself.

_____ is also a synonym for:

- _____ signal; the information about the initial event that is the basis for subsequent modification of the event.
- _____ loop; the causal path that leads from the initial generation of the _____ signal to the subsequent modification of the event.

_____ is a mechanism, process or signal that is looped back to control a system within itself. Such a loop is called a _____ loop.

a. Feedback loop
b. 1990 Clean Air Act
c. Positive feedback
d. Feedback

19. _____ involves establishing specific, measurable and time-targeted objectives. Work on the theory of goal-setting suggests that it's an effective tool for making progress by ensuring that participants in a group with a common goal are clearly aware of what is expected from them if an objective is to be achieved. On a personal level, setting goals is a process that allows people to specify then work towards their own objectives - most commonly with financial or career-based goals.
   a. Resource-based view
   b. Digital strategy
   c. Catfish effect
   d. Goal setting

20. _____ is the use of empirically demonstrated behavior change techniques to improve behavior, such as altering an individual's behaviors and reactions to stimuli through positive and negative reinforcement of adaptive behavior and/or the reduction of maladaptive behavior through punishment and/or therapy.

The first use of the term _____ appears to have been by Edward Thorndike in 1911

   a. 1990 Clean Air Act
   b. Behavior modification
   c. 33 Strategies of War
   d. 28-hour day

21. In operant conditioning, _____ occurs when an event following a response causes an increase in the probability of that response occurring in the future. Response strength can be assessed by measures such as the frequency with which the response is made (for example, a pigeon may peck a key more times in the session), or the speed with which it is made (for example, a rat may run a maze faster.) The environment change contingent upon the response is called a reinforcer.
   a. Diminishing Manufacturing Sources and Material Shortages
   b. Historiometry
   c. Meetings, Incentives, Conferences, and Exhibitions
   d. Reinforcement

22. _____ can be regarded as an outcome of mental processes (cognitive process) leading to the selection of a course of action among several alternatives. Every _____ process produces a final choice. The output can be an action or an opinion of choice.

Chapter 4. Motivation

   a. 28-hour day
   b. 33 Strategies of War
   c. 1990 Clean Air Act
   d. Decision making

23. _____ is the use of consequences to modify the occurrence and form of behavior. _____ is distinguished from classical conditioning (also called respondent conditioning, or Pavlovian conditioning) in that _____ deals with the modification of 'voluntary behavior' or operant behavior. Operant behavior 'operates' on the environment and is maintained by its consequences, while classical conditioning deals with the conditioning of respondent behaviors which are elicited by antecedent conditions.
   a. Unemployment insurance
   b. Outsourcing
   c. Occupational Safety and Health Administration
   d. Operant conditioning

24. _____ refers to training in different ways to improve overall performance. It takes advantage of the particular effectiveness of each training method, while at the same time attempting to neglect the shortcomings of that method by combining it with other methods that address its weaknesses.

Cross training is employee-employer field means, training employees to do one another's work.

   a. 33 Strategies of War
   b. 28-hour day
   c. 1990 Clean Air Act
   d. Cross-training

25. _____ is a habitual pattern of absence from a duty or obligation.

Frequent absence from the workplace may be indicative of poor morale or of sick building syndrome. However, many employers have implemented absence policies which make no distinction between absences for genuine illness and absence for inappropriate reasons.

   a. Emanation of the state
   b. Absenteeism
   c. A4e
   d. A Stake in the Outcome

Chapter 4. Motivation

26. In a human resources context, _____ or labor _____ is the rate at which an employer gains and loses employees. Simple ways to describe it are 'how long employees tend to stay' or 'the rate of traffic through the revolving door.' _____ is measured for individual companies and for their industry as a whole. If an employer is said to have a high _____ relative to its competitors, it means that employees of that company have a shorter average tenure than those of other companies in the same industry.

a. Career portfolios
b. Turnover
c. Ten year occupational employment projection
d. Continuous

27. _____ is an educational process whereby the participant studies their own actions and experience in order to improve performance. This concept is close to learning-by-doing and teaching through examples and repetitions.

_____ is done in conjunction with others, in small groups called _____ sets or two-in, two-out team.

a. A4e
b. A Stake in the Outcome
c. AAAI
d. Action learning

28. A _____ is a business efficiency technique combining the Time Study work of Frederick Winslow Taylor with the Motion Study work of Frank and Lillian Gilbreth (not to be confused with their son, best known through the biographical 1950 film and book Cheaper by the Dozen.) It is a major part of scientific management (Taylorism.)

A _____ would be used to reduce the number of motions in performing a task in order to increase productivity.

a. Total benefits of ownership
b. Time and motion study
c. Prevailing wage
d. Manufacturing operations

29. _____-model (SCOR(r)) is a process reference model developed by the management consulting firm PRTM and AMR Research and endorsed by the Supply-Chain Council (SCC) as the cross-industry de facto standard diagnostic tool for supply chain management. SCOR enables users to address, improve, and communicate supply chain management practices within and between all interested parties in the Extended Enterprise.

SCOR(r) is a management tool, spanning from the supplier's supplier to the customer's customer. The model has been developed by the members of the Council on a volunteer basis to describe the business activities associated with all phases of satisfying a customer's demand.

Chapter 4. Motivation

a. Delayed differentiation
b. Supply chain management software
c. Supply Chain Risk Management
d. Supply-Chain Operations Reference

30. A _____ is a group of employees from various functional areas of the organization - research, engineering, marketing, finance. human resources, and operations, for example - who are all focused on a specific objective and are responsible to work as a team to improve coordination and innovation across divisions and resolve mutual problems.

a. Cross-functional team
b. Sociotechnical systems
c. Goal-setting theory
d. Graduate recruitment

31. _____, a business term, is a measure of how products and services supplied by a company meet or surpass customer expectation. It is seen as a key performance indicator within business and is part of the four perspectives of a Balanced Scorecard.

In a competitive marketplace where businesses compete for customers, _____ is seen as a key differentiator and increasingly has become a key element of business strategy.

a. Customer satisfaction
b. Horizontal integration
c. Foreign ownership
d. Critical Success Factor

32. _____ refers to increasing the spiritual, political, social or economic strength of individuals and communities. It often involves the empowered developing confidence in their own capacities.

The term Human _____ covers a vast landscape of meanings, interpretations, definitions and disciplines ranging from psychology and philosophy to the highly commercialized Self-Help industry and Motivational sciences.

a. Empowerment
b. A Stake in the Outcome
c. AAAI
d. A4e

Chapter 5. Performance Management

1. _____ is a forward looking process for setting goals and regularly checking progress toward achieving those goals. It is a continual feedback process whereby the actual outputs are measured and compared with the desired goals. Any discrepancy or gap is then fed back into changing the inputs of the process, so as to achieve the desired goals or outputs.
    a. 1990 Clean Air Act
    b. 33 Strategies of War
    c. 28-hour day
    d. Performance management

2. There are two types of _____ relationships: formal and informal. Informal relationships develop on their own between partners. Formal _____, on the other hand, refers to assigned relationships, often associated with organizational _____ programs designed to promote employee development or to assist at-risk children and youth.
    a. Fix it twice
    b. Human resource management system
    c. Mentoring
    d. Real Property Administrator

3. _____ describes the situation when output from (or information about the result of) an event or phenomenon in the past will influence the same event/phenomenon in the present or future. When an event is part of a chain of cause-and-effect that forms a circuit or loop, then the event is said to 'feed back' into itself.

    _____ is also a synonym for:

    - _____ signal; the information about the initial event that is the basis for subsequent modification of the event.
    - _____ loop; the causal path that leads from the initial generation of the _____ signal to the subsequent modification of the event.

    _____ is a mechanism, process or signal that is looped back to control a system within itself. Such a loop is called a _____ loop.

    a. Positive feedback
    b. Feedback
    c. Feedback loop
    d. 1990 Clean Air Act

4. _____ involves establishing specific, measurable and time-targeted objectives. Work on the theory of goal-setting suggests that it's an effective tool for making progress by ensuring that participants in a group with a common goal are clearly aware of what is expected from them if an objective is to be achieved. On a personal level, setting goals is a process that allows people to specify then work towards their own objectives - most commonly with financial or career-based goals.

a. Catfish effect
b. Resource-based view
c. Digital strategy
d. Goal setting

5. The _____ captures an expanded spectrum of values and criteria for measuring organizational success: economic, ecological and social. With the ratification of the United Nations and ICLEI _____ standard for urban and community accounting in early 2007, this became the dominant approach to public sector full cost accounting. Similar UN standards apply to natural capital and human capital measurement to assist in measurements required by _____, e.g. the ecoBudget standard for reporting ecological footprint.

a. Triple bottom line
b. 28-hour day
c. 1990 Clean Air Act
d. 33 Strategies of War

6. The general definition of an _____ is an evaluation of a person, organization, system, process, project or product. _____s are performed to ascertain the validity and reliability of information; also to provide an assessment of a system's internal control. The goal of an _____ is to express an opinion on the person / organization/system (etc) in question, under evaluation based on work done on a test basis.

a. Audit committee
b. Audit
c. Internal control
d. A Stake in the Outcome

7.

_____ is a commonly used, yet poorly defined concept in industrial and organizational psychology, the branch of psychology that deals with the workplace. It most commonly refers to whether a person performs their job well. Despite the confusion over how it should be exactly defined, performance is an extremely important criterion that relates to organizational outcomes and success.

a. 28-hour day
b. 33 Strategies of War
c. 1990 Clean Air Act
d. Job performance

8. _____ refers to various methodologies for analyzing the requirements of a job.

The general purpose of _____ is to document the requirements of a job and the work performed. Job and task analysis is performed as a basis for later improvements, including: definition of a job domain; describing a job; developing performance appraisals, selection systems, promotion criteria, training needs assessment, and compensation plans.

   a. Job analysis
   b. Work design
   c. Management process
   d. Hersey-Blanchard situational theory

9. A _____ is a list of the general tasks and responsibilities of a position. Typically, it also includes to whom the position reports, specifications such as the qualifications needed by the person in the job, salary range for the position, etc. A _____ is usually developed by conducting a job analysis, which includes examining the tasks and sequences of tasks necessary to perform the job.
   a. Recruitment
   b. Recruitment advertising
   c. Recruitment Process Insourcing
   d. Job description

10. _____ is a contract between two parties, one being the employer and the other being the employee. An employee may be defined as: 'A person in the service of another under any contract of hire, express or implied, oral or written, where the employer has the power or right to control and direct the employee in the material details of how the work is to be performed.' Black's Law Dictionary page 471 (5th ed. 1979.)
   a. Exit interview
   b. Employment counsellor
   c. Employment
   d. Employment rate

11. _____ is the body of laws, administrative rulings, and precedents which address the legal rights of, and restrictions on, working people and their organizations. As such, it mediates many aspects of the relationship between trade unions, employers and employees. In Canada, employment laws related to unionized workplaces are differentiated from those relating to particular individuals.
   a. Four-day week
   b. Shift work
   c. Trade union
   d. Labor law

Chapter 5. Performance Management   37

12. _____ is the practice of administering written, oral or other tests as a means of determining the suitability or desirability of a job applicant. The premise is that if scores on some test correlate with job performance, then it is economically useful for the employer to select employees based on scores from that test.

As long as there have been employers and employees, employers have looked to various means to pre-qualify applicants for various jobs or positions, or test existing employees to help determine which employee or employees may best qualified for a new position or promotion.

   a. Organizational development
   b. Organizational effectiveness
   c. Organizational culture
   d. Employment testing

13. In operant conditioning, _____ occurs when an event following a response causes an increase in the probability of that response occurring in the future. Response strength can be assessed by measures such as the frequency with which the response is made (for example, a pigeon may peck a key more times in the session), or the speed with which it is made (for example, a rat may run a maze faster.) The environment change contingent upon the response is called a reinforcer.
   a. Historiometry
   b. Reinforcement
   c. Diminishing Manufacturing Sources and Material Shortages
   d. Meetings, Incentives, Conferences, and Exhibitions

14. _____ is a property of a test intended to measure something. The test is said to have _____ if it 'looks like' it is going to measure what it is supposed to measure. For instance, if you prepare a test to measure whether students can perform multiplication, and the people you show it to all agree that it looks like a good test of multiplication ability, you have shown the _____ of your test.
   a. 28-hour day
   b. 33 Strategies of War
   c. 1990 Clean Air Act
   d. Face validity

15. Performance Testing covers a broad range of engineering or functional evaluations where a material, product, system emphasis is on the final measurable performance characteristics.

Performance testing can refer to the assessment of the performance of a human examinee. For example, a behind-the-wheel driving test is a _____ of whether a person is able to perform the functions of a competent driver of an automobile.

Chapter 5. Performance Management

a. Reverse engineering
b. Performance test
c. 28-hour day
d. 1990 Clean Air Act

16. The term _____ in logic applies to arguments or statements.

An argument is valid if and only if the truth of its premises entails the truth of its conclusion, it would be self-contradictory to affirm the premises and deny the conclusion. The corresponding conditional of a valid argument is a logical truth and the negation of its corresponding conditional is a contradiction.

a. Simplification
b. 1990 Clean Air Act
c. Fuzzy logic
d. Validity

17. A _____ is a process in which a potential employee is evaluated by an employer for prospective employment in their company, organization and was established in the late 16th century.

A _____ typically precedes the hiring decision, and is used to evaluate the candidate. The interview is usually preceded by the evaluation of submitted résumés from interested candidates, then selecting a small number of candidates for interviews.

a. Job interview
b. Split shift
c. Payrolling
d. Supported employment

Chapter 5. Performance Management

18. The _____ (Situation, Task, Action, Result) format is a job interview technique used by interviewers to gather all the relevant information about a specific capability that the job requires. This interview format is said to have a higher degree of predictability of future on-the-job performance than the traditional interview.

- Situation: The interviewer wants you to present a recent challenge and situation in which you found yourself.
- Task: What did you have to achieve? The interviewer will be looking to see what you were trying to achieve from the situation.
- Action: What did you do? The interviewer will be looking for information on what you did, why you did it and what were the alternatives.
- Results: What was the outcome of your actions? What did you achieve through your actions and did you meet your objectives. What did you learn from this experience and have you used this learning since?

a. Phrase completion
b. Rasch models
c. STAR
d. Competency-based job descriptions

19. The _____ is a twelve-minute, fifty-question intelligence test used to assess the aptitude of prospective employees for learning and problem-solving in a wide range of occupations. The score is calculated as the number of correct answers given in the allotted time. A score of 20 is intended to indicate average intelligence (corresponding to an intelligence quotient of 100; a rough conversion is accomplished via the following formula: IQ = 2Wonderlic Personnel Test + 60.)

a. 33 Strategies of War
b. Wonderlic Personnel Test
c. 28-hour day
d. 1990 Clean Air Act

20. A _____ is a relatively new executive level position at a corporation, company, organization typically reporting directly to the CEO or board of directors. The _____ is responsible for a brand's image, experience, and promise, and propagating it throughout all aspects of the company. The brand officer oversees marketing, advertising, design, public relations and customer service departments.

a. Director of communications
b. Purchasing manager
c. Chief executive officer
d. Chief brand officer

21. The 'business case for _____', theorizes that in a global marketplace, a company that employs a diverse workforce (both men and women, people of many generations, people from ethnically and racially diverse backgrounds etc.) is better able to understand the demographics of the marketplace it serves and is thus better equipped to thrive in that marketplace than a company that has a more limited range of employee demographics.

An additional corollary suggests that a company that supports the _____ of its workforce can also improve employee satisfaction, productivity and retention.

   a. Virtual team
   b. Diversity
   c. Trademark
   d. Kanban

22. _____ is an advertisement in which a particular product specifically mentions a competitor by name for the express purpose of showing why the competitor is inferior to the product naming it.

This should not be confused with parody advertisements, where a fictional product is being advertised for the purpose of poking fun at the particular advertisement, nor should it be confused with the use of a coined brand name for the purpose of comparing the product without actually naming an actual competitor. ('Wikipedia tastes better and is less filling than the Encyclopedia Galactica.')

In the 1980s, during what has been referred to as the cola wars, soft-drink manufacturer Pepsi ran a series of advertisements where people, caught on hidden camera, in a blind taste test, chose Pepsi over rival Coca-Cola.

   a. 33 Strategies of War
   b. 28-hour day
   c. 1990 Clean Air Act
   d. Comparative advertising

23. _____ is the provision of service to customers before, during and after a purchase.

According to Turban et al. (2002), '_____ is a series of activities designed to enhance the level of customer satisfaction - that is, the feeling that a product or service has met the customer expectation.'

Its importance varies by product, industry and customer; defective or broken merchandise can be exchanged, often only with a receipt and within a specified time frame.

a. 28-hour day
b. 1990 Clean Air Act
c. Service rate
d. Customer service

24. _____ is one of five major domains of personality discovered by psychologists. Openness involves active imagination, aesthetic sensitivity, attentiveness to inner feelings, preference for variety, and intellectual curiosity. A great deal of psychometric research has demonstrated that these qualities are statistically correlated.

   a. Introverts
   b. Openness to experience
   c. Extraversion
   d. Introversion

25. _____ is one of the four elements of marketing mix. An organization or set of organizations (go-betweens) involved in the process of making a product or service available for use or consumption by a consumer or business user.

The other three parts of the marketing mix are product, pricing, and promotion.

   a. Job creation programs
   b. Matching theory
   c. Missing completely at random
   d. Distribution

26. _____ can be regarded as an outcome of mental processes (cognitive process) leading to the selection of a course of action among several alternatives. Every _____ process produces a final choice. The output can be an action or an opinion of choice.

   a. 33 Strategies of War
   b. 1990 Clean Air Act
   c. 28-hour day
   d. Decision making

27. A _____ is a set of categories designed to elicit information about a quantitative or a qualitative attribute. In the social sciences, common examples are the Likert scale and 1-10 _____s in which a person selects the number which is considered to reflect the perceived quality of a product.

A _____ is an instrument that requires the rater to assign the rated object that have numerals assigned to them.

a. Spearman-Brown prediction formula
b. Polytomous Rasch model
c. Thurstone scale
d. Rating scale

28. In finance, an _____ is a contract between a buyer and a seller that gives the buyer the right--but not the obligation--to buy or to sell a particular asset (the underlying asset) at a later day at an agreed price. In return for granting the _____, the seller collects a payment (the premium) from the buyer. A call _____ gives the buyer the right to buy the underlying asset; a put _____ gives the buyer of the _____ the right to sell the underlying asset.
a. A Stake in the Outcome
b. A4e
c. AAAI
d. Option

29. _____ is the use of empirically demonstrated behavior change techniques to improve behavior, such as altering an individual's behaviors and reactions to stimuli through positive and negative reinforcement of adaptive behavior and/or the reduction of maladaptive behavior through punishment and/or therapy.

The first use of the term _____ appears to have been by Edward Thorndike in 1911

a. 33 Strategies of War
b. Behavior modification
c. 1990 Clean Air Act
d. 28-hour day

Chapter 6. Power and Influence 43

1. _____ has been described as the 'process of social influence in which one person can enlist the aid and support of others in the accomplishment of a common task' . A definition more inclusive of followers comes from Alan Keith of Genentech who said '_____ is ultimately about creating a way for people to contribute to making something extraordinary happen.'

_____ is one of the most salient aspects of the organizational context. However, defining _____ has been challenging.

   a. Leadership
   b. 28-hour day
   c. 1990 Clean Air Act
   d. Situational leadership

2. In operant conditioning, _____ occurs when an event following a response causes an increase in the probability of that response occurring in the future. Response strength can be assessed by measures such as the frequency with which the response is made (for example, a pigeon may peck a key more times in the session), or the speed with which it is made (for example, a rat may run a maze faster.) The environment change contingent upon the response is called a reinforcer.
   a. Diminishing Manufacturing Sources and Material Shortages
   b. Meetings, Incentives, Conferences, and Exhibitions
   c. Historiometry
   d. Reinforcement

3. _____ describes the situation when output from (or information about the result of) an event or phenomenon in the past will influence the same event/phenomenon in the present or future. When an event is part of a chain of cause-and-effect that forms a circuit or loop, then the event is said to 'feed back' into itself.

_____ is also a synonym for:

- _____ signal; the information about the initial event that is the basis for subsequent modification of the event.
- _____ loop; the causal path that leads from the initial generation of the _____ signal to the subsequent modification of the event.

_____ is a mechanism, process or signal that is looped back to control a system within itself. Such a loop is called a _____ loop.

   a. Feedback loop
   b. Positive feedback
   c. 1990 Clean Air Act
   d. Feedback

Chapter 6. Power and Influence

4. _____ is one of the managerial functions like planning, organizing, staffing and directing. It is an important function because it helps to check the errors and to take the corrective action so that deviation from standards are minimized and stated goals of the organization are achieved in desired manner. According to modern concepts, _____ is a foreseeing action whereas earlier concept of _____ was used only when errors were detected. _____ in management means setting standards, measuring actual performance and taking corrective action.

    a. Control
    b. Schedule of reinforcement
    c. Turnover
    d. Decision tree pruning

5. _____ is individual power based on a high level of identification with, admiration of, or respect for the powerholder.

Nationalism, Patriotism, Celebrities and well-respected people are examples of _____ in effect.

_____ is one of the Five Bases of Social Power, as defined by Bertram Raven and his colleagues[1] in 1959.

    a. 33 Strategies of War
    b. Referent power
    c. 1990 Clean Air Act
    d. 28-hour day

6. The 'business case for _____', theorizes that in a global marketplace, a company that employs a diverse workforce (both men and women, people of many generations, people from ethnically and racially diverse backgrounds etc.) is better able to understand the demographics of the marketplace it serves and is thus better equipped to thrive in that marketplace than a company that has a more limited range of employee demographics.

An additional corollary suggests that a company that supports the _____ of its workforce can also improve employee satisfaction, productivity and retention.

    a. Diversity
    b. Virtual team
    c. Kanban
    d. Trademark

7. _____ is a form of social influence. It is the process of guiding people and oneself toward the adoption of an idea, attitude, or action by rational and symbolic (though not always logical) means. It is strategy of problem-solving relying on 'appeals' rather than coercion.

Chapter 6. Power and Influence

a. Social loafing
b. Self-enhancement
c. Personal space
d. Persuasion

8. _____ is used to assign the available resources in an economic way. It is part of resource management.

In strategic planning,is a plan for using available resources, for example human resources, especially in the near term, to achieve goals for the future.

a. 28-hour day
b. 1990 Clean Air Act
c. Resource allocation
d. 33 Strategies of War

9. _____ occurs when an individual's thoughts or actions are affected by other people. _____ takes many forms and can be seen in conformity, socialization, peer pressure, obedience, leadership, persuasion, sales, and marketing. Harvard psychologist, Herbert Kelman identified three broad varieties of _____.

a. Soft skill
b. Social awareness
c. Role conflict
d. Social influence

10. _____ is a concept from the field of social psychology that is commonly used to describe the predisposition that individuals have 'to distort self-appraisals so as to maintain the most favorable self-view'. _____ involves sustaining and augmenting a positive view of the self; specifically, people are likely to over-emphasize favorable evaluations of themselves, while they are inclined to minimize or forget critical assessments of themselves. In addition, the concept of _____ suggests that people tend to look for flattering evaluations from others concerning their achievements and talents.

a. Self-enhancement
b. Machiavellianism
c. Persuasion
d. Social loafing

11. In retail sales, a _____ is a form of fraud in which the party putting forth the fraud lures in customers by advertising a product or service at an unprofitably low price, then reveals to potential customers that the advertised good is not available but that a substitute is. This term has lots of other meanings, even outside of the marketing sense.

The goal of the _____ is to convince some buyers to purchase the substitute good as a means of avoiding disappointment over not getting the bait, or as a way to recover sunk costs expended to try to obtain the bait.

 a. 33 Strategies of War
 b. 28-hour day
 c. 1990 Clean Air Act
 d. Bait and switch

12. _____ is a compliance tactic that involves getting a person to agree to a large request by first setting them up by having that person agree to a modest request.

In an early study, a team of psychologists telephoned housewives in California and asked if the women would answer a few questions about the household products they used. Three days later, the psychologists called again.

 a. 33 Strategies of War
 b. 1990 Clean Air Act
 c. 28-hour day
 d. Foot-in-the-door technique

13. The _____ is a fallacy in which someone prematurely claims that an idea or proposal is correct or superior, exclusively because it is new and modern. In a controversy between status quo and new inventions, an _____ argument isn't in itself a valid argument. The fallacy may take two forms: overestimating the new and modern, prematurely and without investigation assuming it to be best-case, or underestimating status quo, prematurely and without investigation assuming it to be worst-case.
 a. A Stake in the Outcome
 b. A4e
 c. AAAI
 d. Appeal to novelty

14. _____ appeal to common practice, argumentum ad antiquitatem, false induction is a common logical fallacy in which a thesis is deemed correct on the basis that it correlates with some past or present tradition. The appeal takes the form of 'this is right because we've always done it this way.'

An _____ essentially makes two assumptions:

- The old way of thinking was proven correct when introduced. In actuality this may be false -- the tradition might be entirely based on incorrect grounds.
- The past justifications for the tradition are still valid at present. In cases where circumstances have changed, this assumption may be false.

The opposite of an _____ is an appeal to novelty, claiming something is good because it is new.

- 'Our society has always ridden horses. It would be foolish to start driving cars.'

    Rebuttal: we want to travel farther and horses are no longer adequate for traveling such great distances. Furthermore, there was a point in our past where our ancestors made the change from walking to riding horses.

- 'Your invention is a bad idea because it has no historical precedent.'

    Rebuttal: the fact that something has not been previously attempted does not guarantee it will fail. Moreover, there is a first time for everything.

a. AAAI
b. Appeal to tradition
c. A Stake in the Outcome
d. A4e

15. _____ refers to the long-term management of intractable conflicts. It is the label for the variety of ways by which people handle grievances--standing up for what they consider to be right and against what they consider to be wrong. Those ways include such diverse phenomena as gossip, ridicule, lynching, terrorism, warfare, feuding, genocide, law, mediation, and avoidance.
    a. 33 Strategies of War
    b. 1990 Clean Air Act
    c. Conflict management
    d. 28-hour day

16. Various _____ can be employed dependent on the culture of the business, the nature of the task, the nature of the workforce and the personality and skills of the leaders. This idea was further developed by Robert Tannenbaum and Warren H. Schmidt (1958, 1973) who argued that the style of leadership is dependent upon the prevailing circumstance; therefore leaders should exercise a range of leadership styles and should deploy them as appropriate.

Chapter 6. Power and Influence

An Autocratic or authoritarian manager makes all the decisions, keeping the information and decision making among the senior management.

a. Management styles
b. 1990 Clean Air Act
c. 28-hour day
d. 33 Strategies of War

17. _____ is both the conscious and unconscious act of revealing more about ourselves to others. This may include but is not limited to thoughts, feelings, aspirations, goals, failures, successes, fears, dreams as well as our likes, dislikes, and favorites. Many people attempt to avoid 'self-disclosing' too much to coworkers, or when dating for fear of being judged negatively by others.

a. Soft skill
b. Social influence
c. Social network analysis
d. Self-disclosure

18. _____ is an educational process whereby the participant studies their own actions and experience in order to improve performance. This concept is close to learning-by-doing and teaching through examples and repetitions.

_____ is done in conjunction with others, in small groups called _____ sets or two-in, two-out team.

a. AAAI
b. A4e
c. A Stake in the Outcome
d. Action learning

19. _____ is a dynamic of being mutually and physically responsible to and sharing a common set of principles with others. This concept differs distinctly from 'dependence' in that an interdependent relationship implies that all participants are emotionally, economically, ecologically and or morally 'interdependent.' Some people advocate freedom or independence as a sort of ultimate good; others do the same with devotion to one's family, community, or society. _____ recognizes the truth in each position and weaves them together.

a. A Stake in the Outcome
b. A4e
c. AAAI
d. Interdependence

Chapter 6. Power and Influence   49

20. _____ is a term used to classify a group leadership theories that inquire the interactions between leaders and followers. A transactional leader focuses more on a series of 'transactions'. This person is interested in looking out for oneself, having exchange benefits with their subordinates and clarify a sense of duty with rewards and punishments to reach goals.
   a. Transactional leadership
   b. 28-hour day
   c. 33 Strategies of War
   d. 1990 Clean Air Act

21. Contingency leadership theory in organizational studies is a type of leadership theory, leadership style, and leadership model that presumes that different leadership styles are contingent to different situations. It is also referred as _____ Â® theory although, as originally convened, the situational theory term is much more restrictive. The original situational theory argues that the best type of leadership is totally determined by the situational variables. Currently there are many styles of leadership.
   a. 28-hour day
   b. Situational leadership
   c. Situational theory
   d. 1990 Clean Air Act

Chapter 7. Leadership

1. _____ has been described as the 'process of social influence in which one person can enlist the aid and support of others in the accomplishment of a common task' . A definition more inclusive of followers comes from Alan Keith of Genentech who said '_____ is ultimately about creating a way for people to contribute to making something extraordinary happen.'

_____ is one of the most salient aspects of the organizational context. However, defining _____ has been challenging.

   a. 1990 Clean Air Act
   b. 28-hour day
   c. Situational leadership
   d. Leadership

2. Contingency leadership theory in organizational studies is a type of leadership theory, leadership style, and leadership model that presumes that different leadership styles are contingent to different situations. It is also referred as _____ ® theory although, as originally convened, the situational theory term is much more restrictive. The original situational theory argues that the best type of leadership is totally determined by the situational variables.Currently there are many styles of leadership.
   a. 28-hour day
   b. Situational theory
   c. 1990 Clean Air Act
   d. Situational leadership

3. The _____ captures an expanded spectrum of values and criteria for measuring organizational success: economic, ecological and social. With the ratification of the United Nations and ICLEI _____ standard for urban and community accounting in early 2007, this became the dominant approach to public sector full cost accounting. Similar UN standards apply to natural capital and human capital measurement to assist in measurements required by _____, e.g. the ecoBudget standard for reporting ecological footprint.
   a. Triple bottom line
   b. 28-hour day
   c. 1990 Clean Air Act
   d. 33 Strategies of War

4. _____ is a leadership style that defines as leadership that creates voluble and positive change in the followers. A transformational leader focuses on 'transforming' others to help each other, to look out for each other, be encouraging, harmonious, and look out for the organization as a whole. In this leadership, the leader enhances the motivation, moral and performance of his follower group.

a. Strong-Campbell Interest Inventory
b. Transformational leadership
c. SESAMO
d. Polynomial conjoint measurement

5. _____ is a term used to classify a group leadership theories that inquire the interactions between leaders and followers. A transactional leader focuses more on a series of 'transactions'. This person is interested in looking out for oneself, having exchange benefits with their subordinates and clarify a sense of duty with rewards and punishments to reach goals.

a. Transactional leadership
b. 33 Strategies of War
c. 1990 Clean Air Act
d. 28-hour day

6. _____ is a 'policy by which management devotes its time to investigating only those situations in which actual results differ significantly from planned results. The idea is that management should spend its valuable time concentrating on the more important items (such as shaping the company's future strategic course.) Attention is given only to material deviations requiring investigation.'

It is not entirely synonymous with the concept of exception management in that it describes a policy where absolute focus is on exception management, in contrast to moderate application of exception management.

a. Trustee
b. Business philosophy
c. C-A-K-E
d. Management by exception

7. The _____ (Situation, Task, Action, Result) format is a job interview technique used by interviewers to gather all the relevant information about a specific capability that the job requires. This interview format is said to have a higher degree of predictability of future on-the-job performance than the traditional interview.

- Situation: The interviewer wants you to present a recent challenge and situation in which you found yourself.
- Task: What did you have to achieve? The interviewer will be looking to see what you were trying to achieve from the situation.
- Action: What did you do? The interviewer will be looking for information on what you did, why you did it and what were the alternatives.
- Results: What was the outcome of your actions? What did you achieve through your actions and did you meet your objectives. What did you learn from this experience and have you used this learning since?

a. Competency-based job descriptions
b. Phrase completion
c. Rasch models
d. Star

8. _____ refers to a range of skills, tools, and techniques used to manage time when accomplishing specific tasks, projects and goals. This set encompass a wide scope of activities, and these include planning, allocating, setting goals, delegation, analysis of time spent, monitoring, organizing, scheduling, and prioritizing. Initially _____ referred to just business or work activities, but eventually the term broadened to include personal activities also.

a. Time management
b. Voice of the customer
c. Formula for Change
d. Cash cow

9. _____ describes the situation when output from (or information about the result of) an event or phenomenon in the past will influence the same event/phenomenon in the present or future. When an event is part of a chain of cause-and-effect that forms a circuit or loop, then the event is said to 'feed back' into itself.

_____ is also a synonym for:

- _____ signal; the information about the initial event that is the basis for subsequent modification of the event.
- _____ loop; the causal path that leads from the initial generation of the _____ signal to the subsequent modification of the event.

_____ is a mechanism, process or signal that is looped back to control a system within itself. Such a loop is called a _____ loop.

a. Positive feedback
b. 1990 Clean Air Act
c. Feedback loop
d. Feedback

10. In contrast, positive feedback is a feedback in which the system responds in the same direction as the perturbation, resulting in amplification of the original signal instead of stabilizing the signal. A positive feedback of 100% or greater will result in a runaway situation. Both positive and _____ require a feedback loop to operate.

a. Feedback loop
b. Negative feedback
c. Positive feedback
d. 1990 Clean Air Act

11.

_____ is a commonly used, yet poorly defined concept in industrial and organizational psychology, the branch of psychology that deals with the workplace. It most commonly refers to whether a person performs their job well. Despite the confusion over how it should be exactly defined, performance is an extremely important criterion that relates to organizational outcomes and success.

a. 28-hour day
b. 1990 Clean Air Act
c. 33 Strategies of War
d. Job performance

12. _____, in psychology, are goals that are achieved by the contribution and co-operation of two or more people, with individual goals that are normally in opposition to each other, working together.

Muzafer Sherif (1954) performed a study involving a group of boys at a camp that were in opposition to one another, one named Eagles, one named the Rattlers, in a zero-sum situation. The opposing groups had strong negative feelings towards each other, resulting in hostile actions such as 'garbage wars'.

a. 28-hour day
b. 33 Strategies of War
c. Superordinate goals
d. 1990 Clean Air Act

13. _____ are a special type of work behavior that are defined as individual behaviors that are beneficial to the organization and are discretionary, not directly or explicitly recognized by the formal reward system. These behaviors are rather a matter of personal choice, such that their omission are not generally understood as punishable. _____ are thought to have an important impact on the effectiveness and efficiency of work teams and organizations, therefore contributing to the overall productivity of the organization.

a. Organizational citizenship behaviors
b. AAAI
c. A Stake in the Outcome
d. A4e

Chapter 7. Leadership

14. The _____ refers to situations in which students perform better than other students simply because they are expected to do so. The effect is named after George Bernard Shaw's play Pygmalion, in which a professor makes a bet that he can teach a poor flower girl to speak and act like an upper-class lady, and is successful.

The _____ requires a student to internalize the expectations of their superiors.

   a. Distinction bias
   b. Halo effect
   c. Confirmation bias
   d. Pygmalion effect

15. A _____ is a prediction that directly or indirectly causes itself to become true, by the very terms of the prophecy itself, due to positive feedback between belief and behavior. Although examples of such prophecies can be found in literature as far back as ancient Greece and ancient India, it is 20th-century sociologist Robert K. Merton who is credited with coining the expression '_____' and formalizing its structure and consequences. In his book Social Theory and Social Structure, Merton gives as a feature of the _____:

In other words, a prophecy declared as truth when it is actually false may sufficiently influence people, either through fear or logical confusion, so that their reactions ultimately fulfill the once-false prophecy.

   a. 1990 Clean Air Act
   b. Self-fulfilling prophecy
   c. 33 Strategies of War
   d. 28-hour day

16. _____ is an educational process whereby the participant studies their own actions and experience in order to improve performance. This concept is close to learning-by-doing and teaching through examples and repetitions.

_____ is done in conjunction with others, in small groups called _____ sets or two-in, two-out team.

   a. AAAI
   b. A Stake in the Outcome
   c. A4e
   d. Action learning

17. There are two types of _____ relationships: formal and informal. Informal relationships develop on their own between partners. Formal _____, on the other hand, refers to assigned relationships, often associated with organizational _____ programs designed to promote employee development or to assist at-risk children and youth.

a. Human resource management system
b. Mentoring
c. Real Property Administrator
d. Fix it twice

Chapter 8. Team Effectiveness and Diversity

1. _____ refers to metrics and measures of output from production processes, per unit of input. Labor _____, for example, is typically measured as a ratio of output per labor-hour, an input. _____ may be conceived of as a metrics of the technical or engineering efficiency of production.
   a. Master production schedule
   b. Remanufacturing
   c. Value engineering
   d. Productivity

2. _____ is a civil designation for persons who are incorporated in a fixed or permanent way to a society or group: regular member of the working staff, permanent staff distinguished from a supernumerary.

   The term '_____' and its counterpart, 'supernumerary,' originated in Spanish and Latin American academy and government; it is now also used in countries all over the world, such as France, the U.S., England, Italy, etc.

   There are _____ members of surgical organizations, of universities, of gastronomical associations, etc.

   a. Numerary
   b. Affiliation
   c. Adam Smith
   d. Abraham Harold Maslow

3. _____-model (SCOR(r)) is a process reference model developed by the management consulting firm PRTM and AMR Research and endorsed by the Supply-Chain Council (SCC) as the cross-industry de facto standard diagnostic tool for supply chain management. SCOR enables users to address, improve, and communicate supply chain management practices within and between all interested parties in the Extended Enterprise.

   SCOR(r) is a management tool, spanning from the supplier's supplier to the customer's customer. The model has been developed by the members of the Council on a volunteer basis to describe the business activities associated with all phases of satisfying a customer's demand.

   a. Delayed differentiation
   b. Supply chain management software
   c. Supply Chain Risk Management
   d. Supply-Chain Operations Reference

4. The 'business case for _____', theorizes that in a global marketplace, a company that employs a diverse workforce (both men and women, people of many generations, people from ethnically and racially diverse backgrounds etc.) is better able to understand the demographics of the marketplace it serves and is thus better equipped to thrive in that marketplace than a company that has a more limited range of employee demographics.

An additional corollary suggests that a company that supports the _____ of its workforce can also improve employee satisfaction, productivity and retention.

a. Trademark
b. Kanban
c. Virtual team
d. Diversity

5. The general definition of an _____ is an evaluation of a person, organization, system, process, project or product. _____s are performed to ascertain the validity and reliability of information; also to provide an assessment of a system's internal control. The goal of an _____ is to express an opinion on the person / organization/system (etc) in question, under evaluation based on work done on a test basis.
   a. A Stake in the Outcome
   b. Internal control
   c. Audit committee
   d. Audit

6. _____ is a concept in ethics with several meanings. It is often used synonymously with such concepts as responsibility, answerability, enforcement, blameworthiness, liability and other terms associated with the expectation of account-giving. As an aspect of governance, it has been central to discussions related to problems in both the public and private (corporation) worlds.
   a. Usury
   b. A4e
   c. A Stake in the Outcome
   d. Accountability

7. _____ is the study of groups, and also a general term for group processes. Relevant to the fields of psychology, sociology, and communication studies, a group is two or more individuals who are connected to each other by social relationships. Because they interact and influence each other, groups develop a number of dynamic processes that separate them from a random collection of individuals.
   a. 1990 Clean Air Act
   b. Collective action
   c. 28-hour day
   d. Group dynamics

8. _____ is a dynamic of being mutually and physically responsible to and sharing a common set of principles with others. This concept differs distinctly from 'dependence' in that an interdependent relationship implies that all participants are emotionally, economically, ecologically and or morally 'interdependent.' Some people advocate freedom or independence as a sort of ultimate good; others do the same with devotion to one's family, community, or society. _____ recognizes the truth in each position and weaves them together.
   a. Interdependence
   b. AAAI
   c. A Stake in the Outcome
   d. A4e

9. _____ is the process by which a new idea or new product is accepted by the market. The rate of _____ is the speed that the new idea spreads from one consumer to the next. Adoption is similar to _____ except that it deals with the psychological processes an individual goes through, rather than an aggregate market process.
   a. Mass marketing
   b. Diffusion
   c. Value chain
   d. Category management

10. _____ is a social phenomenon which tends to occur in groups of people above a certain critical size when responsibility is not explicitly assigned. This phenomenon rarely ever occurs in small groups. In tests, groups of three or fewer, everyone in the group took action as opposed to groups of over ten where in almost every test, no one took action.
    a. Psychological statistics
    b. Diffusion of responsibility
    c. Psychometrics
    d. Groupthink

11. _____ was first described by Barry M. Staw in his 1976 paper, 'Knee deep in the big muddy: A study of escalating commitment to a chosen course of action'. More recently the term Sunk cost fallacy has been used to describe the phenomenon where people justify increased investment in a decision, based on the cumulative prior investment, despite new evidence suggesting that the decision was probably wrong. Such investment may include money, time, or -- in the case of military strategy -- human lives.
    a. Open Options
    b. A Stake in the Outcome
    c. A4e
    d. Escalation of commitment

Chapter 8. Team Effectiveness and Diversity

12. _____ is the change (processing) of information in any manner detectable by an observer. As such, it is a process which describes everything which happens (changes) in the universe, from the falling of a rock (a change in position) to the printing of a text file from a digital computer system. In the latter case, an information processor is changing the form of presentation of that text file.
    a. AAAI
    b. A Stake in the Outcome
    c. A4e
    d. Information processing

13. In the social psychology of groups, _____ is the phenomenon of people making less effort to achieve a goal when they work in a group than when they work alone. This is seen as one of the main reasons groups are sometimes less productive than the combined performance of their members working as individuals.

    • Ringelmann, Max : 1913

    Research began in 1913 with Max Ringelmann's study. He found that when he asked a group of men to pull on a rope, that they did not pull as hard, or put as much effort into the activity, as they did when they were pulling alone.

    a. Machiavellianism
    b. Self-enhancement
    c. Social loafing
    d. Personal space

14. In economics, collective bargaining, psychology, and political science, 'free riders' are those who consume more than their fair share of a public resource, or shoulder less than a fair share of the costs of its production. Free riding is usually considered to be an economic 'problem' only when it leads to the non-production or under-production of a public good (and thus to Pareto inefficiency), or when it leads to the excessive use of a common property resource. The _____ is the question of how to limit free riding (or its negative effects) in these situations.
    a. 28-hour day
    b. Natural monopoly
    c. 1990 Clean Air Act
    d. Free rider problem

15. _____ is a type of thought exhibited by group members who try to minimize conflict and reach consensus without critically testing, analyzing, and evaluating ideas. Individual creativity, uniqueness, and independent thinking are lost in the pursuit of group cohesiveness, as are the advantages of reasonable balance in choice and thought that might normally be obtained by making decisions as a group. During _____, members of the group avoid promoting viewpoints outside the comfort zone of consensus thinking.

a. Psychological statistics
b. Diffusion of responsibility
c. Self-report inventory
d. Groupthink

16. The _____ is a paradox in which a group of people collectively decide on a course of action that is counter to the preferences of any of the individuals in the group. It involves a common breakdown of group communication in which each member mistakenly believes that their own preferences are counter to the group's and, therefore, does not raise objections.
   a. AAAI
   b. Abilene paradox
   c. A Stake in the Outcome
   d. A4e

17. In game theory, an _____ is a set of moves or strategies taken by the players, or their payoffs resulting from the actions or strategies taken by all players. The two are complementary in that given knowledge of the set of strategies of all players, the final state of the game is known, as are any relevant payoffs. In a game where chance or a random event is involved, the _____ is not known from only the set of strategies, but is only realized when the random event(s) are realized.
   a. A4e
   b. AAAI
   c. A Stake in the Outcome
   d. Outcome

18. _____ has been described as the 'process of social influence in which one person can enlist the aid and support of others in the accomplishment of a common task'. A definition more inclusive of followers comes from Alan Keith of Genentech who said '_____ is ultimately about creating a way for people to contribute to making something extraordinary happen.'

_____ is one of the most salient aspects of the organizational context. However, defining _____ has been challenging.

   a. 28-hour day
   b. 1990 Clean Air Act
   c. Situational leadership
   d. Leadership

19. In economics, the term _____ refers to situations where the advancement of a qualified person within the hierarchy of an organization is stopped at a lower level because of some form of discrimination, most commonly sexism or racism, but since the term was coined, '_____' has also come to describe the limited advancement of the deaf, blind, disabled, aged and sexual minorities. It is an unofficial, invisible barrier that prevents women and minorities from advancing in businesses.

This situation is referred to as a 'ceiling' as there is a limitation blocking upward advancement, and 'glass' (transparent) because the limitation is not immediately apparent and is normally an unwritten and unofficial policy. This invisible barrier continues to exist, even though there are no explicit obstacles keeping minorities from acquiring advanced job positions - there are no advertisements that specifically say 'no minorities hired at this establishment', nor are there any formal orders that say 'minorities are not qualified' - but they do lie beneath the surface.

a. 33 Strategies of War
b. 1990 Clean Air Act
c. 28-hour day
d. Glass ceiling

20. _____ is a term used to describe any moral, political that stresses human interdependence and the importance of a collective, rather than the importance of separate individuals. Collectivists focus on community and society, and seek to give priority to group goals over individual goals. The philosophical underpinnings of _____ are for some related to holism or organicism - the view that the whole is greater than the sum of its parts/pieces.

a. Collaborative methods
b. 1990 Clean Air Act
c. Collectivism
d. 28-hour day

21. Engineering _____ is the permissible limit of variation in

1. a physical dimension,
2. a measured value or physical property of a material, manufactured object, system, or service,
3. other measured values (such as temperature, humidity, etc.)
4. in engineering and safety, a physical distance or space (_____), as in a truck (lorry), train or boat under a bridge as well as a train in a tunnel

Dimensions, properties, or conditions may vary within certain practical limits without significantly affecting functioning of equipment or a process. _____s are specified to allow reasonable leeway for imperfections and inherent variability without compromising performance.

The _____ may be specified as a factor or percentage of the nominal value, a maximum deviation from a nominal value, an explicit range of allowed values, be specified by a note or published standard with this information, or be implied by the numeric accuracy of the nominal value. _____ can be symmetrical, as in 40±0.1, or asymmetrical, such as 40+0.2/−0.1.

 a. Tolerance
 b. Zero defects
 c. Quality assurance
 d. Root cause analysis

22. _____, commonly abbreviated to Gen X, is a term used to refer to a generational cohort of children born after the baby boom ended and usually prior to the 1980s

The term _____ has been used in demography, the social sciences, and marketing, though it is most often used in popular culture.

In the U.S. _____ was originally referred to as the 'baby bust' generation because of the drop in the birth rate following the baby boom.

 a. Abraham Harold Maslow
 b. Affiliation
 c. Generation X
 d. Adam Smith

23. _____ is a set of values based on hard work and diligence. It is also a belief in the moral benefit of work and its ability to enhance character. An example would be the Protestant _____.
 a. 33 Strategies of War
 b. 28-hour day
 c. Work ethic
 d. 1990 Clean Air Act

24. The _____ assessment is a psychometric questionnaire designed to measure psychological preferences in how people perceive the world and make decisions.[1] These preferences were extrapolated from the typological theories originated by Carl Gustav Jung, as published in his 1921 book Psychological Types . The original developers of the personality inventory were Katharine Cook Briggs and her daughter, Isabel Briggs Myers. They began creating the indicator during World War II, believing that a knowledge of personality preferences would help women who were entering the industrial workforce for the first time identify the sort of war-time jobs where they would be 'most comfortable and effective'.[xiii] The initial questionnaire grew into the _____, which was first published in 1962.

a. 1990 Clean Air Act
b. Myers-Briggs Type Indicator
c. 33 Strategies of War
d. 28-hour day

25. _____ is an educational process whereby the participant studies their own actions and experience in order to improve performance. This concept is close to learning-by-doing and teaching through examples and repetitions.

_____ is done in conjunction with others, in small groups called _____ sets or two-in, two-out team.

a. Action learning
b. A Stake in the Outcome
c. AAAI
d. A4e

26. In decision theory and estimation theory, the _____ of an estimator, $\hat{\theta}$, of an unknown parameter of the distribution, θ, is the expected value of the loss function

$$R(\theta, \hat{\theta}) = \mathbb{E}_\theta L(\theta, \hat{\theta}) = \int L(\theta, \hat{\theta})\, dP_\theta.$$

where dP_θ is a probability measure parametrized by θ.

- For a scalar parameter θ and a quadratic loss function,

$$L(\theta, \hat{\theta}) = (\theta - \hat{\theta})^2$$

the _____ function becomes the mean squared error of the estimate,

$$R(\theta, \hat{\theta}) = E_\theta(\theta - \hat{\theta})^2$$

- In density estimation, the unknown parameter is probability density itself. The loss function is typically chosen to be a norm in an appropriate function space. For example, for L^2 norm,

$$L(f, \hat{f}) = \|f - \hat{f}\|_2^2$$

the _____ function becomes the mean integrated squared error

$$R(f, \hat{f}) = E\|f - \hat{f}\|^2$$

a. Financial modeling
b. Risk aversion
c. Linear model
d. Risk

27. _____ involves establishing specific, measurable and time-targeted objectives. Work on the theory of goal-setting suggests that it's an effective tool for making progress by ensuring that participants in a group with a common goal are clearly aware of what is expected from them if an objective is to be achieved. On a personal level, setting goals is a process that allows people to specify then work towards their own objectives - most commonly with financial or career-based goals.
a. Resource-based view
b. Catfish effect
c. Digital strategy
d. Goal setting

28. A _____ -- also known as a geographically dispersed team -- is a group of individuals who work across time, space, and organizational boundaries with links strengthened by webs of communication technology. They have complementary skills and are committed to a common purpose, have interdependent performance goals, and share an approach to work for which they hold themselves mutually accountable. Geographically dispersed teams allow organizations to hire and retain the best people regardless of location.

    a. Trademark
    b. Risk management
    c. Virtual team
    d. Kanban

Chapter 9. Conflict and Negotiation

1. _____ refers to the long-term management of intractable conflicts. It is the label for the variety of ways by which people handle grievances--standing up for what they consider to be right and against what they consider to be wrong. Those ways include such diverse phenomena as gossip, ridicule, lynching, terrorism, warfare, feuding, genocide, law, mediation, and avoidance.
   a. 28-hour day
   b. 1990 Clean Air Act
   c. 33 Strategies of War
   d. Conflict management

2. The _____ refers to situations in which students perform better than other students simply because they are expected to do so. The effect is named after George Bernard Shaw's play Pygmalion, in which a professor makes a bet that he can teach a poor flower girl to speak and act like an upper-class lady, and is successful.

   The _____ requires a student to internalize the expectations of their superiors.

   a. Pygmalion effect
   b. Halo effect
   c. Confirmation bias
   d. Distinction bias

3. The _____ is the identical or similar social positions and social roles as a whole that influence the individuals of a group. The _____ of an individual is the culture that he or she was educated and/or lives in, and the people and institutions with whom the person interacts. A given _____ is likely to create a feeling of solidarity amongst its members, who are more likely to keep together, trust and help one another.
   a. 33 Strategies of War
   b. 1990 Clean Air Act
   c. 28-hour day
   d. Social environment

4. _____ is a range of processes aimed at alleviating or eliminating sources of conflict. The term '_____' is sometimes used interchangeably with the term dispute resolution or alternative dispute resolution. Processes of _____ generally include negotiation, mediation and diplomacy.
   a. 28-hour day
   b. 33 Strategies of War
   c. 1990 Clean Air Act
   d. Conflict resolution

Chapter 9. Conflict and Negotiation

5. _____ describes the situation when output from (or information about the result of) an event or phenomenon in the past will influence the same event/phenomenon in the present or future. When an event is part of a chain of cause-and-effect that forms a circuit or loop, then the event is said to 'feed back' into itself.

_____ is also a synonym for:

- _____ signal; the information about the initial event that is the basis for subsequent modification of the event.
- _____ loop; the causal path that leads from the initial generation of the _____ signal to the subsequent modification of the event.

_____ is a mechanism, process or signal that is looped back to control a system within itself. Such a loop is called a _____ loop.

a. Positive feedback
b. 1990 Clean Air Act
c. Feedback loop
d. Feedback

6. _____ is a civil designation for persons who are incorporated in a fixed or permanent way to a society or group: regular member of the working staff, permanent staff distinguished from a supernumerary.

The term '_____' and its counterpart, 'supernumerary,' originated in Spanish and Latin American academy and government; it is now also used in countries all over the world, such as France, the U.S., England, Italy, etc.

There are _____ members of surgical organizations, of universities, of gastronomical associations, etc.

a. Abraham Harold Maslow
b. Numerary
c. Affiliation
d. Adam Smith

7. _____-model (SCOR(r)) is a process reference model developed by the management consulting firm PRTM and AMR Research and endorsed by the Supply-Chain Council (SCC) as the cross-industry de facto standard diagnostic tool for supply chain management. SCOR enables users to address, improve, and communicate supply chain management practices within and between all interested parties in the Extended Enterprise.

SCOR(r) is a management tool, spanning from the supplier's supplier to the customer's customer. The model has been developed by the members of the Council on a volunteer basis to describe the business activities associated with all phases of satisfying a customer's demand.

Chapter 9. Conflict and Negotiation

a. Supply-Chain Operations Reference
b. Supply Chain Risk Management
c. Supply chain management software
d. Delayed differentiation

8. In game theory and economic theory, _____ describes a situation in which a participant's gain or loss is exactly balanced by the losses or gains of the other participant(s.) If the total gains of the participants are added up, and the total losses are subtracted, they will sum to zero. _____ can be thought of more generally as constant sum where the benefits and losses to all players sum to the same value of money and pride and dignity.

a. 33 Strategies of War
b. 28-hour day
c. 1990 Clean Air Act
d. Zero-sum

9. _____ is one of the four elements of marketing mix. An organization or set of organizations (go-betweens) involved in the process of making a product or service available for use or consumption by a consumer or business user.

The other three parts of the marketing mix are product, pricing, and promotion.

a. Job creation programs
b. Missing completely at random
c. Distribution
d. Matching theory

10. _____ is a recursive process where two or more people or organizations work together in an intersection of common goals -- for example, an intellectual endeavor that is creative in nature--by sharing knowledge, learning and building consensus. _____ does not require leadership and can sometimes bring better results through decentralization and egalitarianism. In particular, teams that work collaboratively can obtain greater resources, recognition and reward when facing competition for finite resources._____ is also present in opposing goals exhibiting the notion of adversarial _____, though this is not a common case for using the term.

a. Collectivism
b. Collaboration
c. 28-hour day
d. 1990 Clean Air Act

11. Various _____ can be employed dependent on the culture of the business, the nature of the task, the nature of the workforce and the personality and skills of the leaders. This idea was further developed by Robert Tannenbaum and Warren H. Schmidt (1958, 1973) who argued that the style of leadership is dependent upon the prevailing circumstance; therefore leaders should exercise a range of leadership styles and should deploy them as appropriate.

An Autocratic or authoritarian manager makes all the decisions, keeping the information and decision making among the senior management.

   a. 33 Strategies of War
   b. Management styles
   c. 28-hour day
   d. 1990 Clean Air Act

12. _____, in psychology, are goals that are achieved by the contribution and co-operation of two or more people, with individual goals that are normally in opposition to each other, working together.

Muzafer Sherif (1954) performed a study involving a group of boys at a camp that were in opposition to one another, one named Eagles, one named the Rattlers, in a zero-sum situation. The opposing groups had strong negative feelings towards each other, resulting in hostile actions such as 'garbage wars'.

   a. 28-hour day
   b. 1990 Clean Air Act
   c. 33 Strategies of War
   d. Superordinate goals

13. The _____ captures an expanded spectrum of values and criteria for measuring organizational success: economic, ecological and social. With the ratification of the United Nations and ICLEI _____ standard for urban and community accounting in early 2007, this became the dominant approach to public sector full cost accounting. Similar UN standards apply to natural capital and human capital measurement to assist in measurements required by _____, e.g. the ecoBudget standard for reporting ecological footprint.

   a. 33 Strategies of War
   b. 1990 Clean Air Act
   c. Triple bottom line
   d. 28-hour day

14. In negotiation theory, the _____ or BATNA is the course of action that will be taken by a party if the current negotiations fail and an agreement cannot be reached. BATNA is the key focus and the driving force behind a successful negotiator. BATNA should not be confused with the reservation point or walkaway point.

a. 28-hour day
b. Getting to Yes
c. Best alternative to a negotiated agreement
d. 1990 Clean Air Act

15. In finance, an _____ is a contract between a buyer and a seller that gives the buyer the right--but not the obligation-- to buy or to sell a particular asset (the underlying asset) at a later day at an agreed price. In return for granting the _____, the seller collects a payment (the premium) from the buyer. A call _____ gives the buyer the right to buy the underlying asset; a put _____ gives the buyer of the _____ the right to sell the underlying asset.

a. AAAI
b. A4e
c. A Stake in the Outcome
d. Option

16. The 'business case for _____', theorizes that in a global marketplace, a company that employs a diverse workforce (both men and women, people of many generations, people from ethnically and racially diverse backgrounds etc.) is better able to understand the demographics of the marketplace it serves and is thus better equipped to thrive in that marketplace than a company that has a more limited range of employee demographics.

An additional corollary suggests that a company that supports the _____ of its workforce can also improve employee satisfaction, productivity and retention.

a. Trademark
b. Kanban
c. Virtual team
d. Diversity

17. _____ has been described as the 'process of social influence in which one person can enlist the aid and support of others in the accomplishment of a common task'. A definition more inclusive of followers comes from Alan Keith of Genentech who said '_____ is ultimately about creating a way for people to contribute to making something extraordinary happen.'

_____ is one of the most salient aspects of the organizational context. However, defining _____ has been challenging.

a. 1990 Clean Air Act
b. Leadership
c. Situational leadership
d. 28-hour day

18. _____ can be regarded as an outcome of mental processes (cognitive process) leading to the selection of a course of action among several alternatives. Every _____ process produces a final choice. The output can be an action or an opinion of choice.
   a. 28-hour day
   b. Decision making
   c. 1990 Clean Air Act
   d. 33 Strategies of War

19. In operant conditioning, _____ occurs when an event following a response causes an increase in the probability of that response occurring in the future. Response strength can be assessed by measures such as the frequency with which the response is made (for example, a pigeon may peck a key more times in the session), or the speed with which it is made (for example, a rat may run a maze faster.) The environment change contingent upon the response is called a reinforcer.
   a. Historiometry
   b. Diminishing Manufacturing Sources and Material Shortages
   c. Reinforcement
   d. Meetings, Incentives, Conferences, and Exhibitions

20. _____, a form of alternative dispute resolution (ADR) or 'appropriate dispute resolution', aims to assist two (or more) disputants in reaching an agreement. The parties themselves determine the conditions of any settlements reached-- rather than accepting something imposed by a third party. The disputes may involve (as parties) states, organizations, communities, individuals or other representatives with a vested interest in the outcome.
   a. Meritor Savings Bank v. Vinson
   b. Foreign Corrupt Practices Act
   c. Mediation
   d. Maximum medical improvement

21. _____ is a term that refers both to:

   - a formal discipline used to help appraise, or assess, the case for a project or proposal, which itself is a process known as project appraisal; and
   - an informal approach to making decisions of any kind.

Chapter 9. Conflict and Negotiation

Under both definitions the process involves, whether explicitly or implicitly, weighing the total expected costs against the total expected benefits of one or more actions in order to choose the best or most profitable option. The formal process is often referred to as either CBA (_____) or BCost-benefit analysis

A hallmark of CBA is that all benefits and all costs are expressed in money terms, and are adjusted for the time value of money, so that all flows of benefits and flows of project costs over time (which tend to occur at different points in time) are expressed on a common basis in terms of their 'present value.' Closely related, but slightly different, formal techniques include Cost-effectiveness analysis, Economic impact analysis, Fiscal impact analysis and Social Return on Investment(SROI) analysis. The latter builds upon the logic of _____, but differs in that it is explicitly designed to inform the practical decision-making of enterprise managers and investors focused on optimising their social and environmental impacts.

a. Kepner-Tregoe
b. Decision engineering
c. Gittins index
d. Cost-benefit analysis

Chapter 10. Making Change

1. _____ is a structured approach to transitioning individuals, teams, and organizations from a current state to a desired future state. The current definition of _____ includes both organizational _____ processes and individual _____ models, which together are used to manage the people side of change.

A number of models are available for understanding the transitioning of individuals through the phases of _____ and strengthening organizational development initiative in both government and corporate sectors.

   a. 33 Strategies of War
   b. 1990 Clean Air Act
   c. 28-hour day
   d. Change management

2. _____ of the learning curve effect and the closely related experience curve effect express the relationship between equations for experience and efficiency or between efficiency gains and investment in the effort. The experience of 'learning curves' was first observed by the 19th Century German psychologist Hermann Ebbinghaus according to the difficulty of memorizing varying numbers of verbal stimuli, and subsequent learning about the complex processes of learning are discussed in the

.

The rule used for representing the learning curve effect states that the more times a task has been performed, the less time will be required on each subsequent iteration.

   a. Distribution
   b. Models
   c. Point biserial correlation coefficient
   d. Spatial Decision Support Systems

3. _____ has been described as the 'process of social influence in which one person can enlist the aid and support of others in the accomplishment of a common task' . A definition more inclusive of followers comes from Alan Keith of Genentech who said '_____ is ultimately about creating a way for people to contribute to making something extraordinary happen.'

_____ is one of the most salient aspects of the organizational context. However, defining _____ has been challenging.

   a. 28-hour day
   b. 1990 Clean Air Act
   c. Situational leadership
   d. Leadership

Chapter 10. Making Change

4. _____ is an influential development in the field of social science. It provides a framework for looking at the factors (forces) that influence a situation, originally social situations. It looks at forces that are either driving movement toward a goal (helping forces) or blocking movement toward a goal (hindering forces.)

   a. Force field analysis
   b. Logistics management
   c. Board of governors
   d. Dynamic Enterprise Modeling

5. In physics, and more specifically kinematics, _____ is the change in velocity over time. Because velocity is a vector, it can change in two ways: a change in magnitude and/or a change in direction. In one dimension, _____ is the rate at which something speeds up or slows down.

   a. AAAI
   b. Acceleration
   c. A4e
   d. A Stake in the Outcome

6. A _____ is an alliance among individuals or groups, during which they cooperate in joint action, each in his own self-interest, joining forces together for a common cause. This alliance may be temporary or a matter of convenience. A _____ thus differs from a more formal covenant.

   a. 33 Strategies of War
   b. 1990 Clean Air Act
   c. 28-hour day
   d. Coalition

7. _____ refers to increasing the spiritual, political, social or economic strength of individuals and communities. It often involves the empowered developing confidence in their own capacities.

   The term Human _____ covers a vast landscape of meanings, interpretations, definitions and disciplines ranging from psychology and philosophy to the highly commercialized Self-Help industry and Motivational sciences.

   a. A4e
   b. Empowerment
   c. AAAI
   d. A Stake in the Outcome

Chapter 10. Making Change

8. _____ is one of the managerial functions like planning, organizing, staffing and directing. It is an important function because it helps to check the errors and to take the corrective action so that deviation from standards are minimized and stated goals of the organization are achieved in desired manner. According to modern concepts, _____ is a foreseeing action whereas earlier concept of _____ was used only when errors were detected. _____ in management means setting standards, measuring actual performance and taking corrective action.
   a. Turnover
   b. Schedule of reinforcement
   c. Decision tree pruning
   d. Control

9. _____ is an idea in the field of Organizational studies and management which describes the psychology, attitudes, experiences, beliefs and Values (personal and cultural values) of an organization. It has been defined as 'the specific collection of values and norms that are shared by people and groups in an organization and that control the way they interact with each other and with stakeholders outside the organization.'

This definition continues to explain organizational values also known as 'beliefs and ideas about what kinds of goals members of an organization should pursue and ideas about the appropriate kinds or standards of behavior organizational members should use to achieve these goals. From organizational values develop organizational norms, guidelines or expectations that prescribe appropriate kinds of behavior by employees in particular situations and control the behavior of organizational members towards one another.'

_____ is not the same as corporate culture.

   a. Organizational development
   b. Union shop
   c. Organizational effectiveness
   d. Organizational culture

10. In probability theory, a probability distribution is called _____ if its cumulative distribution function is _____. This is equivalent to saying that for random variables X with the distribution in question, Pr[X = a] = 0 for all real numbers a, i.e.: the probability that X attains the value a is zero, for any number a. If the distribution of X is _____ then X is called a _____ random variable.
    a. Decision tree pruning
    b. Pay Band
    c. Connectionist expert systems
    d. Continuous

11. When an animal's surroundings are controlled, its behavior patterns after reinforcement become predictable, even for very complex behavior patterns. A schedule of reinforcement is the protocol for determining when responses or behaviors will be reinforced, ranging from _____, in which every response is reinforced, and extinction, in which no response is reinforced. Between these extremes is intermittent or partial reinforcement where only some responses are reinforced.
   a. Clinical decision support systems
   b. Continuous reinforcement
   c. Pension System
   d. Recognition-primed decision

12. In business and economics, _____ is a business resource assessment tool enabling a company to compare its actual performance with its potential performance. At its core are two questions: 'Where are we?' and 'Where do we want to be?' If a company or organization is under-utilizing its current resources or is forgoing investment in capital or technology, then it may be producing or performing at a level below its potential. This concept is similar to the base case of being below one's production possibilities frontier.
   a. Cross-selling
   b. Yield management
   c. Gap analysis
   d. Business networking

13. A _____ is a professional who provides advice in a particular area of expertise such as management, accountancy, the environment, entertainment, technology, law , human resources, marketing, medicine, finance, economics, public affairs, communication, engineering, sound system design, graphic design, or waste management.

    A _____ is usually an expert or a professional in a specific field and has a wide knowledge of the subject matter. A _____ usually works for a consultancy firm or is self-employed, and engages with multiple and changing clients.

   a. 1990 Clean Air Act
   b. Consultant
   c. 33 Strategies of War
   d. 28-hour day

14. In operant conditioning, _____ occurs when an event following a response causes an increase in the probability of that response occurring in the future. Response strength can be assessed by measures such as the frequency with which the response is made (for example, a pigeon may peck a key more times in the session), or the speed with which it is made (for example, a rat may run a maze faster.) The environment change contingent upon the response is called a reinforcer.

a. Historiometry
b. Meetings, Incentives, Conferences, and Exhibitions
c. Diminishing Manufacturing Sources and Material Shortages
d. Reinforcement

15. _____ is a concept in ethics with several meanings. It is often used synonymously with such concepts as responsibility, answerability, enforcement, blameworthiness, liability and other terms associated with the expectation of account-giving. As an aspect of governance, it has been central to discussions related to problems in both the public and private (corporation) worlds.
a. A Stake in the Outcome
b. Usury
c. Accountability
d. A4e

16. The general definition of an _____ is an evaluation of a person, organization, system, process, project or product. _____s are performed to ascertain the validity and reliability of information; also to provide an assessment of a system's internal control. The goal of an _____ is to express an opinion on the person / organization/system (etc) in question, under evaluation based on work done on a test basis.
a. Internal control
b. Audit committee
c. A Stake in the Outcome
d. Audit

17. The _____ is a performance management tool for measuring whether the smaller-scale operational activities of a company are aligned with its larger-scale objectives in terms of vision and strategy.

By focusing not only on financial outcomes but also on the operational, marketing and developmental inputs to these, the _____ helps provide a more comprehensive view of a business, which in turn helps organizations act in their best long-term interests. This tool is also being used to address business response to climate change and greenhouse gas emissions.

a. Middle management
b. Management development
c. Commercial management
d. Balanced scorecard

Chapter 10. Making Change

18. _____ describes the situation when output from (or information about the result of) an event or phenomenon in the past will influence the same event/phenomenon in the present or future. When an event is part of a chain of cause-and-effect that forms a circuit or loop, then the event is said to 'feed back' into itself.

   _____ is also a synonym for:

   - _____ signal; the information about the initial event that is the basis for subsequent modification of the event.
   - _____ loop; the causal path that leads from the initial generation of the _____ signal to the subsequent modification of the event.

   _____ is a mechanism, process or signal that is looped back to control a system within itself. Such a loop is called a _____ loop.

   a. Feedback
   b. 1990 Clean Air Act
   c. Feedback loop
   d. Positive feedback

19. _____ is the state or fact of exclusive rights and control over property, which may be an object, land/real estate or intellectual property. An _____ right is also referred to as title. The concept of _____ has existed for thousands of years and in all cultures.
   a. Emanation of the state
   b. A4e
   c. A Stake in the Outcome
   d. Ownership

20. _____ is an organizational development process or philosophy that engages individuals within an organizational system in its renewal, change and focused performance.

   _____ was adopted from work done by earlier action research theorists and practitioners and further developed by David Cooperrider of Case Western Reserve University. It is now a commonly accepted practice in the evaluation of organizational development strategy and implementation of organizational effectiveness tactics.

   a. Appreciative inquiry
   b. AAAI
   c. A4e
   d. A Stake in the Outcome

Chapter 10. Making Change

21. _____ is a recursive process where two or more people or organizations work together in an intersection of common goals -- for example, an intellectual endeavor that is creative in nature--by sharing knowledge, learning and building consensus. _____ does not require leadership and can sometimes bring better results through decentralization and egalitarianism. In particular, teams that work collaboratively can obtain greater resources, recognition and reward when facing competition for finite resources._____ is also present in opposing goals exhibiting the notion of adversarial _____, though this is not a common case for using the term.
   a. 28-hour day
   b. 1990 Clean Air Act
   c. Collaboration
   d. Collectivism

22. _____ refers to the long-term management of intractable conflicts. It is the label for the variety of ways by which people handle grievances--standing up for what they consider to be right and against what they consider to be wrong. Those ways include such diverse phenomena as gossip, ridicule, lynching, terrorism, warfare, feuding, genocide, law, mediation, and avoidance.
   a. Conflict management
   b. 33 Strategies of War
   c. 1990 Clean Air Act
   d. 28-hour day

23. Various _____ can be employed dependent on the culture of the business, the nature of the task, the nature of the workforce and the personality and skills of the leaders. This idea was further developed by Robert Tannenbaum and Warren H. Schmidt (1958, 1973) who argued that the style of leadership is dependent upon the prevailing circumstance; therefore leaders should exercise a range of leadership styles and should deploy them as appropriate.

An Autocratic or authoritarian manager makes all the decisions, keeping the information and decision making among the senior management.

   a. 33 Strategies of War
   b. 28-hour day
   c. Management styles
   d. 1990 Clean Air Act

24. As defined by Richard Beckhard, _____ is a planned, top-down, organization-wide effort to increase the organization's effectiveness and health. _____ is achieved through interventions in the organization's 'processes,' using behavioural science knowledge. According to Warren Bennis, _____ is a complex strategy intended to change the beliefs, attitudes, values, and structure of organizations so that they can better adapt to new technologies, markets, and challenges.

a. Organizational structure
b. Organizational culture
c. Informal organization
d. Organizational development

25. _____ is the temporary suspension or permanent termination of employment of an employee or (more commonly) a group of employees for business reasons, such as the decision that certain positions are no longer necessary or a business slow-down or interruption in work. Originally the term '_____' referred exclusively to a temporary interruption in work, as when factory work cyclically falls off. However, in recent times the term can also refer to the permanent elimination of a position.

a. Termination of employment
b. Wrongful dismissal
c. Retirement
d. Layoff

26. A _____ or business method is a collection of related, structured activities or tasks that produce a specific service or product (serve a particular goal) for a particular customer or customers. It often can be visualized with a flowchart as a sequence of activities.

There are three types of _____es:

1. Management processes, the processes that govern the operation of a system. Typical management processes include 'Corporate Governance' and 'Strategic Management'.
2. Operational processes, processes that constitute the core business and create the primary value stream. Typical operational processes are Purchasing, Manufacturing, Marketing, and Sales.
3. Supporting processes, which support the core processes. Examples include Accounting, Recruitment, Technical support.

A _____ begins with a customer's need and ends with a customer's need fulfillment. Process oriented organizations break down the barriers of structural departments and try to avoid functional silos.

a. Business process
b. 33 Strategies of War
c. 28-hour day
d. 1990 Clean Air Act

27. An _____ is a mostly hierarchical concept of subordination of entities that collaborate and contribute to serve one common aim.

Organizations are a variant of clustered entities. The structure of an organization is usually set up in many a styles, dependent on their objectives and ambience.

a. Open shop
b. Organizational development
c. Organizational structure
d. Informal organization

28. The _____ captures an expanded spectrum of values and criteria for measuring organizational success: economic, ecological and social. With the ratification of the United Nations and ICLEI _____ standard for urban and community accounting in early 2007, this became the dominant approach to public sector full cost accounting. Similar UN standards apply to natural capital and human capital measurement to assist in measurements required by _____, e.g. the ecoBudget standard for reporting ecological footprint.
   a. 33 Strategies of War
   b. 1990 Clean Air Act
   c. Triple bottom line
   d. 28-hour day

29. In neuroscience, the _____ is a collection of brain structures which attempts to regulate and control behavior by inducing pleasurable effects.

A psychological reward is a process that reinforces behavior -- something that, when offered, causes a behavior to increase in intensity. Reward is an operational concept for describing the positive value an individual ascribes to an object, behavioral act or an internal physical state.

   a. 33 Strategies of War
   b. 1990 Clean Air Act
   c. Reward system
   d. 28-hour day

30. The term _____ is used in various contexts. For example, in business process modeling the enterprise _____ is often referred to as the business _____. Process models are core concepts in the discipline of Process Engineering.
   a. 33 Strategies of War
   b. 1990 Clean Air Act
   c. 28-hour day
   d. Process model

Chapter 10. Making Change

31. _____ comprises the actual output or results of an organization as measured against its intended outputs (or goals and objectives.)

Specialists in many fields are concerned with _____ including strategic planners, operations, finance, legal, and organizational development.

In recent years, many organizations have attempted to manage _____ using the balanced scorecard methodology where performance is tracked and measured in multiple dimensions such as:

- financial performance (e.g. shareholder return)
- customer service
- social responsibility (e.g. corporate citizenship, community outreach)
- employee stewardship

a. A4e
b. A Stake in the Outcome
c. AAAI
d. Organizational performance

32. _____ is a forward looking process for setting goals and regularly checking progress toward achieving those goals. It is a continual feedback process whereby the actual outputs are measured and compared with the desired goals. Any discrepancy or gap is then fed back into changing the inputs of the process, so as to achieve the desired goals or outputs.
   a. 28-hour day
   b. 33 Strategies of War
   c. Performance Management
   d. 1990 Clean Air Act

33. _____ is something that a firm can do well and that meets the following three conditions:

Competencies are things that companys execute well across several business units or product sectors.

Firms usually have few competencies, but these are usually less liable to change rapidly.

1. It provides consumer benefits
2. It is not easy for competitors to imitate
3. It can be leveraged widely to many products and markets.

A _____ can take various forms, including technical/subject matter know-how, a reliable process and/or close relationships with customers and suppliers (Mascarenhas et al. 1998.)

a. Dominant Design
b. Learning-by-doing
c. Core competency
d. NAIRU

34. _____, also erroneously called Work engagement, is a widely employed, yet poorly defined concept, developed principally from the consulting community. As a result, each consulting firm asserts different definitions of the concept, component elements (commitment, job satisfaction, pride, job commitment, discretionary effort. etc), and resulting business outcomes.
   a. A4e
   b. AAAI
   c. A Stake in the Outcome
   d. Employee engagement

35.

_____ is a commonly used, yet poorly defined concept in industrial and organizational psychology, the branch of psychology that deals with the workplace. It most commonly refers to whether a person performs their job well. Despite the confusion over how it should be exactly defined, performance is an extremely important criterion that relates to organizational outcomes and success.

   a. 1990 Clean Air Act
   b. 28-hour day
   c. 33 Strategies of War
   d. Job performance

36. A _____ is a research instrument consisting of a series of questions and other prompts for the purpose of gathering information from respondents. Although they are often designed for statistical analysis of the responses, this is not always the case. The _____ was invented by Sir Francis Galton.
   a. Questionnaire construction
   b. Mystery shoppers
   c. Structured interview
   d. Questionnaire

37. _____ is an advertisement in which a particular product specifically mentions a competitor by name for the express purpose of showing why the competitor is inferior to the product naming it.

This should not be confused with parody advertisements, where a fictional product is being advertised for the purpose of poking fun at the particular advertisement, nor should it be confused with the use of a coined brand name for the purpose of comparing the product without actually naming an actual competitor. ('Wikipedia tastes better and is less filling than the Encyclopedia Galactica.')

In the 1980s, during what has been referred to as the cola wars, soft-drink manufacturer Pepsi ran a series of advertisements where people, caught on hidden camera, in a blind taste test, chose Pepsi over rival Coca-Cola.

a. 33 Strategies of War
b. 28-hour day
c. 1990 Clean Air Act
d. Comparative advertising

38. _____, cultural quotient or CQ, is a theory within management and organisational psychology, positing that understanding the impact of an individual's cultural background on their behaviour is essential for effective business, and measuring an individual's ability to engage successfully in any environment or social setting. First described by Christopher Earley and Soon Ang in _____: Individual Interactions Across Cultures. The book was published in 2003 by Stanford University.

a. Free cash flow
b. Time to market
c. Cultural intelligence
d. Sole proprietorship

39. A _____ is a process in which a potential employee is evaluated by an employer for prospective employment in their company, organization and was established in the late 16th century.

A _____ typically precedes the hiring decision, and is used to evaluate the candidate. The interview is usually preceded by the evaluation of submitted résumés from interested candidates, then selecting a small number of candidates for interviews.

a. Payrolling
b. Split shift
c. Supported employment
d. Job interview

40. Organizational culture is not the same as _____. It is wider and deeper concepts, something that an organization 'is' rather than what it 'has' (according to Buchanan and Huczynski.)

Chapter 10. Making Change

_____ is the total sum of the values, customs, traditions and meanings that make a company unique.

a. Path-goal theory
b. Work design
c. Job analysis
d. Corporate culture

41. The _____ refers to situations in which students perform better than other students simply because they are expected to do so. The effect is named after George Bernard Shaw's play Pygmalion, in which a professor makes a bet that he can teach a poor flower girl to speak and act like an upper-class lady, and is successful.

The _____ requires a student to internalize the expectations of their superiors.

a. Halo effect
b. Pygmalion effect
c. Distinction bias
d. Confirmation bias

42. The _____ is the identical or similar social positions and social roles as a whole that influence the individuals of a group. The _____ of an individual is the culture that he or she was educated and/or lives in, and the people and institutions with whom the person interacts. A given _____ is likely to create a feeling of solidarity amongst its members, who are more likely to keep together, trust and help one another.

a. 28-hour day
b. 33 Strategies of War
c. 1990 Clean Air Act
d. Social environment

43. _____ can be regarded as an outcome of mental processes (cognitive process) leading to the selection of a course of action among several alternatives. Every _____ process produces a final choice. The output can be an action or an opinion of choice.

a. 33 Strategies of War
b. 28-hour day
c. 1990 Clean Air Act
d. Decision making

Chapter 10. Making Change

44. In the field of human resource management, _____ is the field concerned with organizational activity aimed at bettering the performance of individuals and groups in organizational settings. It has been known by several names, including employee development, human resource development, and learning and development.

Harrison observes that the name was endlessly debated by the Chartered Institute of Personnel and Development during its review of professional standards in 1999/2000.

   a. Performance appraisal
   b. Revolving door syndrome
   c. Person specification
   d. Training and Development

45. _____ is an educational process whereby the participant studies their own actions and experience in order to improve performance. This concept is close to learning-by-doing and teaching through examples and repetitions.

_____ is done in conjunction with others, in small groups called _____ sets or two-in, two-out team.

   a. A Stake in the Outcome
   b. AAAI
   c. A4e
   d. Action learning

46. _____ is a contract between two parties, one being the employer and the other being the employee. An employee may be defined as: 'A person in the service of another under any contract of hire, express or implied, oral or written, where the employer has the power or right to control and direct the employee in the material details of how the work is to be performed.' Black's Law Dictionary page 471 (5th ed. 1979.)

   a. Employment rate
   b. Exit interview
   c. Employment counsellor
   d. Employment

47. The _____ (Situation, Task, Action, Result) format is a job interview technique used by interviewers to gather all the relevant information about a specific capability that the job requires. This interview format is said to have a higher degree of predictability of future on-the-job performance than the traditional interview.

- Situation: The interviewer wants you to present a recent challenge and situation in which you found yourself.
- Task: What did you have to achieve? The interviewer will be looking to see what you were trying to achieve from the situation.
- Action: What did you do? The interviewer will be looking for information on what you did, why you did it and what were the alternatives.
- Results: What was the outcome of your actions? What did you achieve through your actions and did you meet your objectives. What did you learn from this experience and have you used this learning since?

a. Star
b. Competency-based job descriptions
c. Phrase completion
d. Rasch models

48. _____ is how top executives of business corporations are paid. This includes a basic salary, bonuses, shares, options and other company benefits. Over the past three decades, _____ has risen dramatically beyond the rising levels of an average worker's wage.

a. Evidence-based management
b. Association management company
c. Anti-leadership
d. Executive compensation

49. A _____ is a compensation, usually financial, received by a worker in exchange for their labor.

Compensation in terms of _____s is given to worker and compensation in terms of salary is given to employees. Compensation is a monetary benefits given to employees in returns of the services provided by them.

a. Profit-sharing agreement
b. State Compensation Insurance Fund
c. Wage
d. Performance-related pay

50. _____ is the process of comparing the cost, cycle time, productivity, or quality of a specific process or method to another that is widely considered to be an industry standard or best practice. Essentially, _____ provides a snapshot of the performance of your business and helps you understand where you are in relation to a particular standard. The result is often a business case for making changes in order to make improvements.

a. Cost leadership
b. Competitive heterogeneity
c. Complementors
d. Benchmarking

51. A _____ is the belief that there is a technique, method, process, activity, incentive or reward that is more effective at delivering a particular outcome than any other technique, method, process, etc. The idea is that with proper processes, checks, and testing, a desired outcome can be delivered with fewer problems and unforeseen complications. _____s can also be defined as the most efficient (least amount of effort) and effective (best results) way of accomplishing a task, based on repeatable procedures that have proven themselves over time for large numbers of people.
   a. Best practice
   b. Fix it twice
   c. Design management
   d. Hierarchical organization

52. The _____ is given by the United States National Institute of Standards and Technology. Through the actions of the National Productivity Advisory Committee chaired by Jack Grayson, it was established by the Malcolm Baldrige National Quality Improvement Act of 1987 - Public Law 100-107 and named for Malcolm Baldrige, who served as United States Secretary of Commerce during the Reagan administration from 1981 until his 1987 death in a rodeo accident. APQC, , organized the first White House Conference on Productivity, spearheading the creation and design of the _____ in 1987, and jointly administering the award for its first three years.
   a. Scenario planning
   b. Business Network Transformation
   c. Time and attendance
   d. Malcolm Baldrige National Quality Award

53. The U.S. _____ is an independent agency of the United States government which holds primary responsibility for enforcing the federal securities laws and regulating the securities industry, the nation's stock and options exchanges, and other electronic securities markets. The SEC was created by section 4 of the Securities Exchange Act of 1934 (now codified as 15 U.S.C. Â§ 78d and commonly referred to as the 1934 Act.)
   a. 33 Strategies of War
   b. Securities and Exchange Commission
   c. 28-hour day
   d. 1990 Clean Air Act

ANSWER KEY

Chapter 1
1. a   2. d   3. d   4. b   5. d   6. b   7. a   8. d   9. d   10. d
11. b   12. c   13. d   14. d   15. d   16. c   17. d   18. d   19. d   20. d
21. b   22. b   23. d   24. b   25. a   26. d   27. a   28. a

Chapter 2
1. b   2. d   3. d   4. d   5. c   6. d   7. b   8. b   9. c   10. c
11. d

Chapter 3
1. b   2. a   3. a   4. d   5. d   6. d   7. b   8. d   9. b   10. d
11. d   12. d   13. d   14. d   15. d   16. d   17. d   18. d   19. b   20. d
21. d   22. a   23. b   24. d   25. d   26. d   27. d   28. d   29. c   30. d
31. d

Chapter 4
1. d   2. d   3. d   4. d   5. d   6. d   7. c   8. d   9. d   10. d
11. d   12. c   13. d   14. d   15. d   16. b   17. d   18. d   19. d   20. b
21. d   22. d   23. d   24. d   25. b   26. b   27. d   28. b   29. d   30. a
31. a   32. a

Chapter 5
1. d   2. c   3. b   4. d   5. a   6. b   7. d   8. a   9. d   10. c
11. d   12. d   13. b   14. d   15. b   16. d   17. a   18. c   19. b   20. d
21. b   22. d   23. d   24. b   25. d   26. d   27. d   28. d   29. b

Chapter 6
1. a   2. d   3. d   4. a   5. b   6. a   7. d   8. c   9. d   10. a
11. d   12. d   13. d   14. b   15. c   16. a   17. d   18. d   19. d   20. a
21. b

Chapter 7
1. d   2. d   3. a   4. b   5. a   6. d   7. d   8. a   9. d   10. b
11. d   12. c   13. a   14. d   15. b   16. d   17. b

Chapter 8
1. d   2. a   3. d   4. d   5. d   6. d   7. d   8. a   9. b   10. b
11. d   12. d   13. c   14. d   15. d   16. b   17. d   18. d   19. d   20. c
21. a   22. c   23. c   24. b   25. a   26. d   27. d   28. c

Chapter 9
1. d   2. a   3. d   4. d   5. d   6. b   7. a   8. d   9. c   10. b
11. b   12. d   13. c   14. c   15. d   16. d   17. b   18. b   19. c   20. c
21. d

Chapter 10

1. d	2. b	3. d	4. a	5. b	6. d	7. b	8. d	9. d	10. d
11. b	12. c	13. b	14. d	15. c	16. d	17. d	18. a	19. d	20. a
21. c	22. a	23. c	24. d	25. d	26. a	27. c	28. c	29. c	30. d
31. d	32. c	33. c	34. d	35. d	36. d	37. d	38. c	39. d	40. d
41. b	42. d	43. d	44. d	45. d	46. d	47. a	48. d	49. c	50. d
51. a	52. d	53. b